# MINI SAGAS

## Fictional Fun

THE ENGLISH COUNTIES

EDITED BY MARK RICHARDSON
& DONNA SAMWORTH

First published in Great Britain in 2010 by:
Young Writers
Remus House
Coltsfoot Drive
Peterborough
PE2 9JX
Telephone: 01733 890066
Website: www.youngwriters.co.uk


Book Design by Ali Smith & Spencer Hart

SB ISBN 978-0-85739-212-1

# FOREWORD

Young Writers was established in 1990 with the aim of encouraging and nurturing writing skills in young people and giving them the opportunity to see their work in print. By helping them to become more confident and expand their creative skills, we hope our young writers will be encouraged to keep writing as they grow.

School pupils nationwide have been exercising their minds to create their very own short stories, Mini Sagas, using no more than fifty words, to be included here in our latest competition, *The Adventure Starts Here ...*

The entries we received showed an impressive level of creativity and imagination, providing an absorbing look into the eager minds of our future authors.

# YE CONTENTS OF AUTHORS

Congratulations to all young writers who appear in this book

## Copthorne CE Junior School, Crawley



## Crowstone Preparatory School, Southend



## Forest Row CE Primary School



## Geoffrey Field Junior School, Reading



## Hartest CE (VC) Primary School, Bury St Edmunds



## Hothfield Junior School, Silsden

## Isambard Brunel Junior School, Portsmouth



## Langland Community School, Milton Keynes



## Linthorpe Primary School, Middlesbrough



## Maldon Primary School, Maldon

# MINI SAGAS

## THE INTRUDER

Woke with a start, *what was that?* Noises downstairs, heart skipped a beat. Squeaky floorboards moaned as he crept down the stairs, quiet as a mouse. A loud crash, a shatter of glass. Heard swearing downstairs. Faced intruder, old, startled, wrinkled face stared back.
'Hey love, fancy a cuppa?'
'Grandma ...'

Callum Brookes-Duncan (11)

## A FLOWER

A flower is nice to have a look at and smells nice. People have them in their garden or on window sills. They grow from seeds or bulbs then become nice flowers. There are lots of names for flowers like daisies or daffodils. My favourite flowers are roses and tulips.

Katherine Harris (12)

## THE MYSTERIOUS CREATURE

A mysterious, stroppy creature burst the door open with a big crash! Instead of running, I stood up for myself. I would destroy the creature, no matter what. No one would stop me. It couldn't stop me. It came out of the dark ... but it was a unicorn!

Connie McKenzie-Nicholls (8)

## ICARUS AND DAEDALUS

In the prison, where no light shone, Icarus and Daedalus were held because of their knowledge of the labyrinth. They stuck bird feathers with candle wax to make wings to escape. 'Don't fly too near the sun or the wax will melt!' cried Icarus. He did and plummeted to Earth.

Thomas Schofield (10)

## TREASURE CHEST

Alice walked along the shore of the shimmering sea. Surprisingly the fairy princess, Crystal, joined her! Alice found herself helping Crystal find the lost gem! They walked; Crystal decided flying was quicker, so they flew to a chest. As Alice held the gem she awoke, was it all a dream?

Sophie Cook (10)
**Abberley Primary School, Abberley**

## IF THE SHOE FITS

Ella was trudging along the rocky road towards Princess' boarding school - the problem was she hadn't got any posh shoes, all she had were some black boots. When she got to Sapphire dorm, her room mates told her they had spares. She tried them on and they fitted absolutely perfectly.

Beth Grainger (11)
**Abberley Primary School, Abberley**

## THE HEROIC EGG

'Help!' screamed some toast in trouble!
'Don't worry, Wonder Egg is here!'
The heroic egg flew over and tried to save the toast. But the egg's arch enemy Whisk-Man got in his way and the egg fell to the floor becoming just a small scrambled omelette ready to eat.

Charley Enefer (11)
**Abberley Primary School, Abberley**

## THE SHRIMP'S HOLIDAY

One day a tiny, lonely shrimp found a ladybird with a broken wing. He took him to his home and fixed its wing so, he let it go. The caring shrimp got a certificate for helping animals that were hurt. Surprisingly for him he got to be a shrimp vet!

Kimberley Roach (10)
**Abberley Primary School, Abberley**

## THE BUTTERFLY

The delicate, pearly, white butterfly fluttered around a magnificent, beautiful garden which had amber primroses and silvery birch trees, also it had a gorgeous waterfall that tinkled during the day. As the butterfly fluttered up to the waterfall a slimy frog eyed her. And in a flick, she was gone.

Jemima Freudmann (11)

**Abberley Primary School, Abberley**

## WINDOW HERO

There once was a man who was by day a window cleaner, but by night was a Superhero and tonight he was up against Talking Toilets. He got a plunger and stuck it down the Talking Toilet's throat and the Superhero, whose name I cannot reveal, saved the day again.

Lewis Morgan (11)

**Abberley Primary School, Abberley**

## DUCK'S DAY!

Dear Diary. Today was a beautiful day for swimming. I watched the weather channel and the beaches were lovely. So I decided to have a break. On the plane I read my book and I was sick. When I got out I saw people skiing! Yours sincerely, Sir Duck Love.

Hayleigh Wallis (10)

**Abberley Primary School, Abberley**

## HORACE'S DOOMSDAY

Horace plodded along the winding track: Little did he know he was about to be doomed! The forest was dark but Horace the Hedgehog could see perfectly because he loves his carrots. Just then Horace saw a beetle. yummy, but he fell down a fox hole.
'Yum,' said the fox.

Rory Chance (11)

**Abberley Primary School, Abberley**

## STRANGERS!

Midnight. I walked steadily among the narrow streets, cautiously eyeing every corner. Unexpectedly, two men appeared, they put their cold, wrinkly fingers on my shoulders, they had red glowing eyes. I think they were vampires. I didn't dare to blink, they let out a deafening screech ... I woke up.

Hadiyah Ilyas (10)
**All Saint's CE Primary School, Bradford**

## SCARED

The house was creepy. John was all alone. John heard a loud noise. Suddenly he saw a shadow on the doorstep, it was very large. He opened the door and a deadly, horrifying face said, 'Trick or treat?' John shut the door, terrified.

Danyal Hussain (10)
**All Saint's CE Primary School, Bradford**

## FIROON, THE FIRE FOX

I walked out and thought my dog was gone. In front of me was a huge, dull monster. 'I am Firoon the fire fox,' roared the monster. I was terrified. He approached and whispered, 'I am your worst nightmare.'
I woke up and found out that I was just dreaming.

Muhammed Awais (9)

**All Saint's CE Primary School, Bradford**

## THE JOURNEY IN THE RAINFOREST

I was walking through the creepy rainforest. While I was walking, a slithering beast came near me. We both screamed like girls. Impulsively, I ran up to the monster and I strangled its green slimy neck. Then he put its disgusting, wrinkly foot in my mouth. I won the battle.

Adil Hussain (10)

**All Saint's CE Primary School, Bradford**

## THE HAUNTED HOUSE OF TERROR

It was on a Sunday morning when one of my friends dared me to go to the old abandoned house for one hour. So I went right in and sat there. When there were five minutes left, things got strange. I started hearing noises, so I ran out screaming crazily.

Omair Khan (10)

**All Saint's CE Primary School, Bradford**

## THE ADVENTURE OUTSIDE

I went on an adventure outside then I got home. Then I heard a noise in the kitchen, so I went downstairs to see what it was. I was scared. But halfway down I started to scream, because I heard a smash and ran ...

Callum Britton (10)

**All Saint's CE Primary School, Bradford**

## MY ADVENTURE WITH SANTA CLAUS

Lizzie was sleeping soundly until ... she hurried down the stairs, went into her living room and saw - 'Santa Claus?' whispered Lizzie. 'I want to go on your sleigh.'
Santa Claus replied, 'Ho, ho, ho, let's go!'
Lizzie enjoyed flying through the night sky delivering presents.

Hira Ilyas (10)
**All Saint's CE Primary School, Bradford**

## THE ADVENTURE STARTS HERE

One spooky day there lived a girl called Coraline. She was feeling really tired so she went to bed. When she was halfway there the doorbell rang. She went to see who it was. It was a monster and an alien. They said, 'Trick or treat? Sweeties please Madam!'

Natasha Azeem (10)
**All Saint's CE Primary School, Bradford**

## ONCE UPON A TIME

Once upon a time there was a girl called Jennifer. She found a secret passage. She opened the door and she found herself in a magical world. 'Wow! Where am I. I have never seen such a beautiful place before! Am I dreaming?'

Aneesa Hussain (10)

**All Saint's CE Primary School, Bradford**

## THE MARVELLOUS MEDICINE OF GEORGE

Once George decided to make up a medicine for Grandma. He used millions of ingredients. With a mischievous grin on his face he handed it over to Grandma. Then the skinny granny shot up into the sky. Suddenly the petrified gran woke up and screamed. Now she's calm.

Abullah Hayat (10)

**All Saint's CE Primary School, Bradford**

## THE ROTTEN MUM SHOP

'You're mean you cow!' screamed Gemma. Gemma was a stubborn girl. 'I'll take you to the rotten mum shop!' she cackled. At the rotten shop she was given a new mum. 'She's boring, I want my own mum back!' she cried.
'Well tough luck, I've had enough,' said her mum.

Beth Protheroe (9)
**Bardsey Primary School, Bardsey**

## THE FOX AND THE DUCK

One day a man met a wizard. The wizard waved his wand and said you will have a day in the life of a duck. 'Oh no, I'm a duck, I might as well go for a swim.'

He went downstream and got eaten by a fox!

Angus Mackie (9)
**Bardsey Primary School, Bardsey**

## THE THREE LITTLE WOLVES AND THE BIG BAD PIG

One day three little wolves left home. 'Watch out for the big bad pig,' warned Mother.
First they built a house of bricks but the big bad pig knocked it down. 'What shall we do?'
'I know. If we build it from flowers he won't come near, he has hay fever.'

Maisie Archer (9)

**Bardsey Primary School, Bardsey**

## THE EVIL GHOST

One night I opened the door, I saw a dark mysterious man but before I could call the police he flew off. He could float, he was a ghost! He took all my belongings too. Suddenly he came back and taunted me. 'Wahaha,' he said.

Ben Gould (9)

**Bardsey Primary School, Bardsey**

## THE CAMPING TRIP!

One dark night, four friends were camping. Marshmallows were roasting and everything was perfect. Then suddenly Emma saw a huge shadow.
'Oh help, a monster!' she screamed.
Just then her three friends emerged from a bush. 'That shadow was fake! It was just us!'

Molly Russell (9)

**Bardsey Primary School, Bardsey**

## THE SHADOW

One scary night a boy saw a strange shadow that made him quake with fear. He called the Ghostbusters, they arrived there in a flash. They threw open the door and got all their equipment ready and ... *Wham!* The ghost had vanished. He lived happily as a very healthy boy.

Tom Chapman (9)

**Bardsey Primary School, Bardsey**

## BE AWARE OF THE GHOST

The ghost crept into Jacob's house and took his clothes when Jacob was upstairs on his amazing Xbox. The ghost was making scary noises, so Jacob shouted to his neighbour, 'Help[! Help!' The neighbour came round, he helped Jacob look for it, they finally got it and threw it out.

Richard Greenwood (9)

**Bardsey Primary School, Bardsey**

## THERE'S NOTHING WE CAN DO

Humpty Dumpty was strolling through the forest. He realised that he was getting a bit tired, so he sat on a nearby wall and had a long nap. He woke up startled, because he was in two halves and was surrounded by hundreds of soldiers. 'There's nothing we can do.'

Rachel Mawson (9)

**Bardsey Primary School, Bardsey**

## MONSTER MAKER

One dark night in a graveyard the church door flung open, a screaming noise echoed through the church. There was a flash of light. A cyclops was making a monster. The monster came alive. They left the church and began emptying graves to make new monsters to rule the world.

Adam Barstow (9)

**Bardsey Primary School, Bardsey**

## BO PEEP

Bo Peep had lost her sheep, but discovered she knew where they were, well she thought she did! She asked Red Riding Hood if she would help her round the sheep. 'They're not sheep they're clouds, you're not wearing your glasses. Your sheep are in the field!'

Abigail Cookman (9)

**Bardsey Primary School, Bardsey**

## EXECUTION

Suddenly he emerged onto the streets in Ancient Rome! There was excitement all around! It was wonderful. Then he came to a courtyard adorned with a wooden block, he laid his head on it - 'This feels comfortable ...' The last thing he heard was the sound of the axe coming down.

Rupert Poole (10)
**Barton Stacey Primary School, Winchester**

## UNTITLED

It was a dark Christmas when Jake woke up. He thought, *normally they're up by now.* He wandered down the deserted steps, there was a creak, but he walked into the room. There was a gloomy figure and it moved slightly. It groaned and said, 'Merry Christmas.'

Jack Barber (10)
**Barton Stacey Primary School, Winchester**

## INSIDE THE ELEVATOR

In the elevator the doors closed behind, he was stuck. He didn't feel the motion of going up, he pressed the alarm button, but didn't hear an alarm, he felt a sudden shake. Unexpectedly the top of the lift came off and a man said, 'We're just fixing the lift.'

Archie Horobin (10)

**Barton Stacey Primary School, Winchester**

## THE FRIGHTFUL EVENING

Lightning struck on the murky evening street, where there was a black figure. Susan, the hairdresser, saw it stalking to her shop. Its hair was growing outwards and claws poking out of its fingers. It opened the door … 'Can I get a makeover, I'm having a bad hair day!'

Natalie Joyce (10)

**Barton Stacey Primary School, Winchester**

## NIGHTMARE

The misty street was like a nightmare, Chloe was uneasy going home. It looked completely deserted, until ... Chloe was certain she saw a black mysterious figure walking closer and closer towards her. 'Hello!' it shouted, Chloe was terrified. 'I've come to take you home!' Chloe was relieved, it was Dad!

Alice Kitching (10)
**Barton Stacey Primary School, Winchester**

## VEGETABLE VENGEANCE

One morning Farmer Andy was out ploughing, enjoying the fresh air. The blades, vigorously slicing through the moist soil, lay before him. The loud, grunting machine woke vegetable-loving, old Ben as he looked across the garden and frustratedly yelled, 'All this because I beat you in a vegetable competition?'

Daniel Read (11)
**Barton Stacey Primary School, Winchester**

## THE NOISES

Stella switched the TV on and flicked through the channels. Before long she heard a series of bangs, screams and more deafening sounds. She looked out the window, worried and curious. She couldn't see anything so she went outside. She was trembling and her knees shook uncontrollably. More sounds. Fireworks!

Lara Coetzee (10)
**Barton Stacey Primary School, Winchester**

## UNTITLED

Children squealing, adults clinking glasses, whilst roaming amongst the swanky rooms, doors banging by careless children, hiding and seeking. One big crash from excitement below, Tom woke up startled to see not children but angry men in black! He'd been dreaming sweet dreams, but living a nightmare!

Arabella Cutler (11)
**Barton Stacey Primary School, Winchester**

## THE BEAUTIFUL PICTURE

An artist painted a lovely picture with crystal-blue eyes, red lips, beautiful blonde hair, cheeks red as a bloomed rose and a fringe covering her right eye. Fading scars ran down her neck, three centimetres long. 'That's her, that's the killer,' said the witness ...

Harry Barber (10)

**Barton Stacey Primary School, Winchester**

## THE SHADOW

In a deserted room late at night a boy was lying on his bed listening to some music. Suddenly he heard the floor creak and a mysterious shadow appeared. The door slammed open and a figure was standing there. 'Turn your music down now!' his mum exclaimed.

Daniel Bearpark (11)

**Barton Stacey Primary School, Winchester**

## THE KISS

In a deserted field a man saw a lady. His heart fell for her. Not knowing his fate he leant forward to kiss her ... he fell down dead. The lady ran away, blood dripping from her extremely sharp fangs.

Grace Murray (10)
**Barton Stacey Primary School, Winchester**

## PARTY POPPER

The party was unbelievably manic. Jane was having the time of her life. Some strangers walked in. However nobody noticed, they blended into the crowd. Once the party was over, the strangers stayed and got very close to Jane. 'Happy Birthday,' exclaimed her long lost cousins from abroad.

Ryan White (11)
**Barton Stacey Primary School, Winchester**

## SLOPPY VAMPIRE

Richard opened his girlfriend's door. He wanted a sloppy kiss. Rebecca got out of her orange bed and went to him. She opened her mouth. Richard stared at her until he saw her teeth. Rebecca wasn't a girl, she was a vampire.

Kayden Morley (10)
**Barton Stacey Primary School, Winchester**

## FRIGHTFUL FOREST

*Bang!* The door slammed shut. Joe walked down the staircase. At the bottom a door creaked open. He stepped through to a forest. It was eerie, silent, still and cold! Every step it got colder! He'd die if he stayed here! Suddenly he heard a noise, 'Wake up Joe.'

Jasmine McClutchie (9)
**Barton Stacey Primary School, Winchester**

## PICTURE PERFECT

Blood-red luscious lips, nut-brown hair flowing over her shoulders, a long face with a button nose to fit. Ears like butterfly wings fine and dainty with colourful jewels dripping down skimming her elegant neck. The artist turned the finished portrait around. Yes that's the murderer! That's her ...

Charlotte Burgess (11)

**Barton Stacey Primary School, Winchester**

## THE SHOWDOWN!

James had a gun in his pocket and the sheriff had one in his pocket. It was a showdown! The bell rang. It was twelve o'clock. The two guns rang out! Only one hit. The sheriff was dead! Now James is an outlaw.

Aidan Stirrup (10)

**Broadbent Fold Primary School, Dukinfield**

## TV TERROR

One morning a boy woke up from a restless night's sleep and turned on the TV but the TV came alive and ate the boy! But suddenly the boy woke up and it was just a nightmare so he went back to sleep. Or did he?

Brandon Rustidge (10)
**Broadbent Fold Primary School, Dukinfield**

## ALEXANDRA AND HER SCARY SURPRISE

Alexandra walked through the dark, creepy house, she was scared. All the shadows looked like zombies, including hers. She opened the door with a creak. In her room everything had turned into pumpkins, she shouted her mum. Suddenly a witch appeared. 'Help!' shouted Alexandra . . .
It was her mum. 'Happy Halloween.'

Bethany Morgan (7)
**Broadbent Fold Primary School, Dukinfield**

## LOST

It was cold and dark in the dreadful Tower of Doom! Miley was feeling frightened and gloomy. It was terrible and she always had someone to comfort her. She thought about everything that had happened in the tower. It was so scary she wanted to go home, and fast too.

Joan Harris (9)

**Broadbent Fold Primary School, Dukinfield**

## SCAREDY DUCKS!

The pink house stood in haunted silence as Duncan and Faye waddled towards the shattered windows. They flew into its dark depths. They crept into the fourth bedroom and peered through. Suddenly a black figure screamed and fell. It was Mother Duck with brooms and bowls!

Emily Beer (10)

**Broxbourne CE Primary School, Broxbourne**

## BREAKING BONES!

Maisey, the mad child, liked to break bones in her body. She once jumped to the ninth bar on the climbing frame. Not surprisingly she broke her wrist. Mrs Leg rushed to the screaming child, whilst comforting her into the ambulance. Maisey is a disaster waiting to happen! As usual.

Charlotte Elliott (10)

**Broxbourne CE Primary School, Broxbourne**

## THE FUNNY HAPPENING!

Charlotte was a crazy child who always liked to chew her pens. She was chewing her pen. Suddenly she realised that the ink was leaking into her mouth. She rushed into the bathroom to rinse her mouth, as she was she started to giggle ridiculously, she likes doing that too.

Maisey Quinn (10)

**Broxbourne CE Primary School, Broxbourne**

## MRS K

Running out of breath, Grace sprinted past Freya then Ella across the line. The next day, Grace was walking through the lower meadow. Suddenly she saw a dragon, can it be a triple twonk. She frantically raced home. When she was at home she peered through the window and saw ...

Phoebe Walker (10)

**Broxbourne CE Primary School, Broxbourne**

## THE BEST BIRTHDAY PRESENT EVER!

Jasmine was a young adventurous girl. Jasmine really wanted a cute dog, but her parents didn't. It was Jasmine's birthday. She invited her best friend Katie. Katie carried a big heavy cage. Jasmine opened the cage, there was an adorable puppy. Her mum and dad couldn't do anything about it!

Molly Wilson (10)

**Broxbourne CE Primary School, Broxbourne**

## THE WEIRD WORLD

Lily, a young girl, liked climbing trees. One day she entered a mysterious wood filled with gorgeous trees. She decided to climb one of the trees which had a magnificent apple. As she picked the apple the world spun round. With a zap she had figured out, she was animated!

Alexandra Weir (10)

**Broxbourne CE Primary School, Broxbourne**

## JUMPING GENIUS

Lala a young girl liked jumping. Lala decided to jump. She used her pogo stick. Suddenly she jumped so high that she flew into the clouds. Frantically she fell down and landed in an apple tree. At long last she fell off the apple tree. She was surrounded by apples.

Katie Elsom (10)

**Broxbourne CE Primary School, Broxbourne**

## JERMAINE AND THE SOLAR SYSTEM

Jermaine, an intelligent young lad enjoyed the solar system. He invented a whole solar system in the suffocated air of his room. His invention suddenly exploded into miniature sparks of electricity. Suddenly the air no longer hung around the room like an omen. He had destroyed his only desire.

Lewis Rice (9)
**Broxbourne CE Primary School, Broxbourne**

## SHAGGY AND SCOOBY

There was a young boy called Shaggy who had a dog called Scooby. They both went to the shop where something odd happened. A little pug bit open the cash register and gave it to Scooby. He ate the green notes. He ran to Shaggy and gave him a kiss.

Alexander Pook
**Broxbourne CE Primary School, Broxbourne**

## THE MUSKY HOUSE

Jackie rocketed through the woods and into the musky house. The malevolent moon shone through the cracked window. Now she was really scared. She could hear the cries of an old man so she jumped out. She was doomed. He began to choke her. That was the end of Jackie.

Melissa Robbins (10)

**Broxbourne CE Primary School, Broxbourne**

## ME AND THE OMEN

The house was silent, darkness engulfed me. All of a sudden a dark omen grabbed me at once. I tried to escape but death boomed. Suddenly the dark figure fell and plummeted to the ground. I looked around. A window was what I sighted. Finally I escaped. The omen moaned ...

Brett Waldock (10)

**Broxbourne CE Primary School, Broxbourne**

## UNTITLED

The moon hung in the sky like an omen. Tendrils of darkness binded a solitary soul. The underworld broke out in uncivilised chaos. Souls soared over the crumbling buildings veiled in shadows. Demons broke loose into the world which was destroyed. Jack ran in horror. The demon invasion has begun.

Eliot Barrett-Holman (10)

**Broxbourne CE Primary School, Broxbourne**

## KITTENS AT LAST!

Isabelle wished for two small kittens. One day her parents said to her she could get two kittens. When she got there, she saw the cutest kittens, so Isabelle bought them.

When she got home she made so many things for them. Every day she played with them and loved them.

Molly Clark (10)

**Broxbourne CE Primary School, Broxbourne**

## MRS JONES' DAY AT WORK

Mrs Jones snatched her son's piggy bank. She headed to work. She cackled, while paying her lunch with 1 and 2p. Mrs May was not pleased, but Y5 thought it was hysterical. From then on, Mrs Jones decided to behave, until the time came to pay her lunch fees … again!

Kiara Whelan (10)
**Broxbourne CE Primary School, Broxbourne**

## WORLD WAR III

A veil of flames engulfed the massive engine as it plummeted out of the sky! Suddenly the citadel broke out in uncivilised chaos. They feared the Germans would have a mighty weapon of mass destruction, the lethal atomic bomb. They said this was only the beginning of World War III.

Benjamin Hart (10)
**Broxbourne CE Primary School, Broxbourne**

# THE RABBITS IN THE PET SHOP

Molly, a young girl, dreamt for two small rabbits. One day her parents explained that they were going to the pet shop to choose them. She picked a grey one and a white one. When she reached home she played with them and fed them. Molly loved her new rabbits.

Isabelle Keys (10)
**Broxbourne CE Primary School, Broxbourne**

# ELLA VS BOLT

Ella, a young runner, sprinted like a bullet from a gun trying to get to the finish line. Bolt ran straight past her, Ella had to speed up, the wind was smacking her face but she couldn't give up. She sped up and ran straight past Bolt. Ella won, finally.

Freya Wakefield (10)
**Broxbourne CE Primary School, Broxbourne**

## SPIKE'S TRAMPOLINE ADVENTURE

Spike the tortoise walked onto the trampoline. When I came out, Spike was jumping madly on the trampoline. I rushed to the trampoline and tried to drag her off, but she dug her claws into the black surface. It broke as I pulled harder, it fell flat on the floor

Macy Jacob (10)
**Broxbourne CE Primary School, Broxbourne**

## THE DESERTER THAT CAME TO AN END

Freya, a pretty girl, experimented a pretty trendy maker. You take an image of yourself, it turns you into cool. Suddenly her invention overloaded making ugly pictures of Freya. They all fell from the sky. Freya soared into a massive ugly picture that consumed her invention. Freya saved the day.

Ella Jones (10)
**Broxbourne CE Primary School, Broxbourne**

## DARK SPIRIT DEFEATED

Sam rocketed through the derelict forest. The darkness engulfed him. Corpses littered the surface. The dark spirit was close behind. Sam doubled back, the spirit came to an abrupt halt. That's all he needed, Sam jumped out. He thrashed his leg at the spirits temple. He had defeated the omen.

Ollie Trevett (10)
**Broxbourne CE Primary School, Broxbourne**

## CHOWMEIN ATTACKS!

'Hello, my master,' said Chowmein. 'It's alive!' he screamed! Towering over him was a gigantic pile of chowmein. Poised, ready to strike.
'Stop!' boomed a voice. Jamie Oliver swivelled round to stare into the face of a soldier. 'You may kill me, but you will never destroy my Chowmein, ha!'

Robert Norris (10)
**Broxbourne CE Primary School, Broxbourne**

## HAMSTER'S REVENGE

Matt cautiously strolled through the derelict woods as the howling wind engulfed everything around him. Something stirred! Suddenly a huge robo-bionic hamster charged towards him. But he was ready. He quickly dived underneath it as it collided with a tree. Then Matt walked on as if nothing had happened ...

Benjamin Lewis (10)
**Broxbourne CE Primary School, Broxbourne**

## UNTITLED

Mickster, the best biker in the world, loves to experiment. He loves to do radical things on his BMX. One day he went for a 360 and he fell and hurt his wrist. The ambulance came and helped him up, but Mickster soon found out that he didn't break anything.

Grace Neville (10)
**Broxbourne CE Primary School, Broxbourne**

## THE GREAT WHITE

Silently, Alex dived into the sea then he saw the great white's eyes, emotionless orbs. The shark rocketed towards him with tremendous speed. Alex swam quickly up to the water surface with the shark following close behind. He just managed to clamber to the surface, marginally escaping the great white.

Joe Linkson (10)
**Broxbourne CE Primary School, Broxbourne**

## A VAMPIRE'S VISIT

Blood drained from my body. My heart beat its perhaps last beat. Jacob's fangs anchored deeper into my neck. Time was running out. I needed to do something quickly. I hauled all my leftover energy together, it was just enough for a slap, so I slapped Jacob hard. He vanished.

Madeleine Usher (10)
**Broxbourne CE Primary School, Broxbourne**

## SHARK ATTACK

Its black beady eyes darting around for his victim. A haunted silence, the deafening scream from a whale. The shark retreated. When the whale passed him he struck. The whale was dead. The enemy clan Orcas were here. He lashed out, the enemy were threatened. The intensity levels lowered quickly.

Matthew Squires (10)

**Broxbourne CE Primary School, Broxbourne**

## THE FADING MOONLIGHT

The moon was bright, the owls were tweeting, and the road was empty apart from the leaves rustling at the edge of the pavement. At midnight, the bells would ring and the moon would shine brighter. The darkness was more scary than usual, and the graveyard would make weird noises.

Louis Schembri (11)

**Broxbourne CE Primary School, Broxbourne**

## THE MAN!

One bright summer's day I was walking in the forest collecting berries and summer fruits until a man with a chainsaw cut down a huge tree and it nearly fell on me! I ran up to the man and asked, 'Why did you do that?' He had killed me. Dead!

Emma Hutton (10)

**Copthorne CE Junior School, Crawley**

## THE HAUNTED HOUSE!

I once saw an old tattered house. Cobwebs hung from the roof and there was dust on the floor. I opened the creaky door and I saw lots of bats hanging from the ceiling. I walked up the stairs, opened a door and felt a hand touching my back - argh!

James Campbell (9)

**Copthorne CE Junior School, Crawley**

## REBECCA'S GOOD BIRTHDAY

Once upon a time there lived a little girl called Rebecca. One day it was her birthday and she got loads of presents. When it was Sunday she had a party. It was a sleepover party and Evie, Tia, Caitlin and Eleanor came and it was good fun.

Rebecca Heath (8)
**Copthorne CE Junior School, Crawley**

## THE TARAMALTSA

Many years ago there lived a creature called the Taramaltsa. It wandered through deserts and climbed mountains as big as Earth itself. One day the Taramaltsa was sitting on a patch of grass. The grass grew and the Taramaltsa drowned. We remember it by telling this story every hundred years.

Molly Townsend (9)
**Copthorne CE Junior School, Crawley**

## TOP DOG

Jodie looked out of the kitchen window because she heard a noise in the garden. There was a dog, barking. She took the dog to the police station. To her surprise, one week later, she received a reward of £500. It was a valuable show dog. What a shock!

Megan Mortlock (8)
**Crowstone Preparatory School, Southend**

## SHOP SHOCK

'Next!' shouted the cashier. Hannah moved forward. '£9 please,' he said impatiently. Hannah produced three £3 notes. The cashier was astonished. 'I don't believe it,' he gasped.
Just then another customer asked, 'Can you change this £9 note for three threes?' The cashier fainted.

Gabriella Cuba (9)
**Crowstone Preparatory School, Southend**

## THE BREAK IN

Jhon stayed in the house while Jackob went to get some food. Jhon went to get a cup of tea and trod on Jackob's special plate that was on the floor. Because he'd broken it he broke everything else. He knocked the door down and hit himself on the head.

Rebecca Ley (9)
**Crowstone Preparatory School, Southend**

## THE HOUSE THAT GERRY BUILT

I opened the door. It fell off its hinges. I opened the window. It fell out. I pulled the shower curtain. It came down. Then the tap came off in my hand. 'Who built this house?' I shouted.
'A German,' replied my mum.
'That explains a lot ... it's Gerry built.'

Annis Choo (9)
**Crowstone Preparatory School, Southend**

## EGG ON HIS FACE

Dawn and Eve fought. Now they were in an expensive hotel. Over breakfast they fought again. Dawn threw a fried egg sandwich at Eve, who ducked - it hit the manager who made them leave. He got a shock when he learned that the girls' father owned the hotel chain.

Daniella Reeve (9)
**Crowstone Preparatory School, Southend**

## BRAIN CUT

I was watching telly. It suddenly turned off - I threw the remote at it. I sat there for four hours, it went dark. Dad came home. I said, 'There's a power cut.'
'No there's not, the street lights are on.' It was just a fuse.

Finley Hopson (9)
**Crowstone Preparatory School, Southend**

## SWERVING BALLS

Finley and Aaron were watching the World Cup. The commentator was remarking about how this new ball swerved and how the players disliked it. Tevez took a free kick and the ball came straight through the TV screen into their lounge. 'He's right, it does swerve,' exclaimed Aaron.

Aaron Cocks (9)
**Crowstone Preparatory School, Southend**

## THE SHED MYSTERY

Late one night I saw a light in the shed. I crept down the path. I heard a chomping sound coming from inside. Gently pushing open the door I saw … my dad stuffing himself with fish and chips. 'Don't tell Mum,' he said, 'I'm supposed to be on a diet.'

Noah Jordan (9)
**Crowstone Preparatory School, Southend**

# A ROCKET TO EARTH

Once there were two aliens called Megan and Nick. They wanted to go to Earth so they built a rocket and flew all the way there. Nick thought everything was strange. Megan didn't like the food. Nick said he knew another planet - Mars - so they flew the rocket to Mars!

Alicia Massey (8)

**Crowstone Preparatory School, Southend**

# THE CRASH

In a big city there was a little car called Speedy and he had a friend called Vroom. One day they had a race but they did not know that they were on the same track. Then there was a big crash. Then there was a bang and a wallop.

Lucas Drury (8)

**Crowstone Preparatory School, Southend**

## GONE!

Susan walked into the corridor. She stood in the garden. How very mysterious. Susan thought Daniel and Jake said they would be in the garden. 'Daniel, Jake,' she called loudly, 'are you out here?' There was no reply. Maybe they were in the kitchen. They were always in there together.

Abbie Crawford ((8)

**Crowstone Preparatory School, Southend**

## SPIDERS

TJ walked into his room. He saw two red spiders in a corner. Mum would scream if she saw them! She would definitely freak out! TJ hid them in his wardrobe. They would be safe in there. He had a brilliant idea. Tomorrow he would move them to the shed ...

Benjamin Biggs (8)

**Crowstone Preparatory School, Southend**

## SCARED

I walked down the street. *Crack!* I jumped then kept on walking. Suddenly I heard a gigantic bang! I started jogging then a man in a black suit and a red tie started chasing after me. Soon he caught up. I found out it was just my brother!

Daniel Cuba (8)
**Crowstone Preparatory School, Southend**

## THE LONELY CAMEL

The lonely camel walked through the scorching hot desert. He really needed a friend! Suddenly he saw a small round face. It was a little desert rat. 'Hello,' said the camel, 'want to be friends?'
'OK,' said the desert rat. So the lonely, friendly camel was not lonely anymore. Hooray!

Anna Samieh-Tucker (8)
**Crowstone Preparatory School, Southend**

## OH TOM!

Lilly walked into her house with her sister. Suddenly a floating sheet came charging down the stairs going, *whoooooo.*
'Argh!' they both ran round the house like nutters.
*Whoooooo* it went.
Lilly's legs came to a halt. She turned around. 'Tom!' The duvet had fallen off! 'Oh Tom!' they shouted.

Chloe Forster (8)
**Crowstone Preparatory School, Southend**

## IT

Megan walked along glancing back, it was still there, she paced, it did as well. She couldn't hold it in, she ran, not looking back. She swung the door open to her house, she ran into the kitchen, grabbed a knife and confronted it, darkness surrounded her, it stood staring.

Fine Minns (11)
**Forest Row CE Primary School**

## THE NIGHTMARE

The camping troop had been resting in the woods when *they* came. Lumbering beasts with contorted faces, huge boils fit to burst with pus and grotesquely obese.
'Run!' shouted the group leader. They set off at a run with the apparent zombies in hot pursuit. Wake up John!

Sidney Ellis (11)
**Forest Row CE Primary School**

## THE DEAD

The temperature was unbelievably hot as Dan stepped slowly through the desert. He was holding his happy goldfish in a bag of water. Slowly he became dehydrated. Suddenly, a bloodthirsty snake slid out of nowhere and bit Dan with its venomous fangs. He died miserably. The fish died too.

Isabel Dieleman (10)
**Forest Row CE Primary School**

## WHEN THEY CAME

The groaning, the constant groaning. The clawing, the constant clawing, they wouldn't stop, they were hungry for flesh. Sid had a pan. Set fire to the gas tank in the factory to stop the bloodshed. He sprinted to the tank, made a fuse, lit it and ran, boom gone.

Alexander Muggeridge (10)

**Forest Row CE Primary School**

## HOPE GONE

Jamie knew he shouldn't do that but he just had to keep digging, trying to escape with his friend Brono. They had to find, Brono's dad. They were almost free when *bang!* Gunfire! Jamie collapsed dead. Brono surrendered, but it was too late. *Bang!*

Eddie Saunders (10)

**Forest Row CE Primary School**

## THE TERROR

Liz's legs felt like lead as she tried to sprint away. Heavy footsteps thundered behind her, closing in every second. Undergrowth tore at her legs. Suddenly a stone cold hand grasped her shoulder, sending a shiver down her spine. Within seconds the gun was pointing at her heart. Then ... *bang!*

Amber Walton (11)

**Forest Row CE Primary School**

## FOOD POISONING

Nick ate a roast pheasant and didn't feel so good. His mum took him to the doctors, he had food poisoning. He went home and got in bed. Holly came round to see what was going on. She gave Nick the kiss of life. Nick jumped out of bed.

Oliver Spackman (10)

**Forest Row CE Primary School**

## THE ATTACK OF THE CROCODILE

Far away in Australia the cameraman Jack raced his vehicle towards a lion kill to film.
Unfortunately on the way he had to cross a river. When he got to the middle of the river, his land rover started to sink. Unfortunately Jack got eaten by a crocodile!

Glen Chandler (11)

**Forest Row CE Primary School**

## THE CRACKER OF DOOM

As Willow walked down her road, on her way back from school, she remembered her dream of talking crackers, she could never hear what they were saying, but their mouths moved. She opened the gate to her garden, and there, on the swing was a cracker.
'Hello!' said the cracker.

Lily O'Gorman (11)

**Forest Row CE Primary School**

## THE FOLLOWER

Kerry's heart hammered in her chest. Shadows engulfed her. She was alone. Suddenly she whipped round in terror, she was being followed. A silver glint flashed in the darkness. Kerry tried to scream, but no noise came out, only a trickle of thick red blood staining the grass.

Jacqueline Du Bled (11)
**Forest Row CE Primary School**

## A DEPRESSING DAY IN THE LIFE OF NICK

There wasn't much time for Nick. He ran and ran frantically but he knew he wasn't going to make it. He sat on a bench, crying his eyes out. Meanwhile Holly Douch had just got married to Nathan Wilkins. Nick knew he had missed out on a lifetime opportunity!

Nick Martin (11)
**Forest Row CE Primary School**

## DANI AWAKEN

Dani gazed up dizzily as she woke. Her vision was blurred and faded; she saw a strange, distorted creature looming over her. It murmured and burbled, unmistakably like a different language or even an alien! The beast yawned sleepily, Dani knew it was only her mum. 'Phew!' Relieved, Dani sighed.

Freya Harris (10)
**Forest Row CE Primary School**

## THE SHADOWS

There was a mystical moor with a dying person rolling on the floor. Through the foggy paths you could see green glowing light shaped like a castle. Suddenly the moon turned around with an evil face, through the mist you can hear a wolf shouting 'Aooo'. Suddenly the person cried.

Connor Evans-Perry (9)
**Geoffrey Field Junior School, Reading**

## ENCHANTED TOADSTOOL

Once upon a time there was an enchanted land. There was a toadstool temple, it had golden toadstools growing up it. All of a sudden there were people attacking the temple, snip, cut, and a giant kaboom! Then someone came and got the people and they were absolutely gone forever.

Alyssa Farmbrough (9)
**Geoffrey Field Junior School, Reading**

## PIXIE PATH

The colossal castle stood surrounded by glamorous pixies in the land. One day the pixies were playing in the pond. They didn't notice a wizard sneak in the castle. They saw a puff of smoke. With a click of a finger they were in the castle and defeated the wizard …

Caitlyn Murray (9)
**Geoffrey Field Junior School, Reading**

## THE SWEET SHOP

In Tiptree there was a sweet shop. Its name was Lovely Sweets. The owners were a giant snail and evil rabbit. However lovely wasn't the word. One day a boy called Sam brought some chocolate and after one bite, shrank. Snail and Rabbit had tricked him. 'Got you!' they laughed.

Scarlet Broughton (9)

**Hartest CE (VC) Primary School, Bury St Edmunds**

## THE VALLEY OF HORROR

Once there was a dragon that ruled a land for 3 years until a knight came along and said to everyone, 'I will kill the dragon.' He went to the dragon and killed it. The dragon was no more. They were free again. Then the knight went back home.

Charlie Ives (9)

**Hartest CE (VC) Primary School, Bury St Edmunds**

## CHELSEA VS LIVERPOOL

Chelsea are two up and Kakuta, the newest player, is warming up. They're taking their best player off. They said he needs a rest. Now he's on. Lampard the awesome free-kick taker has a shot, it hits the crossbar, bounces back to Kaktuta and *goal.* What a goal.

Benjamin Turner (8)
**Hartest CE (VC) Primary School, Bury St Edmunds**

## IN THE LIFE OF A POLICEMAN

A mounted policeman was chasing a robber. The robber climbed up a tree. Then he fell on to the back of a police horse then the horse kicked him in to the back of a police van and the robber was taken to court.

George Brega (9)
**Hartest CE (VC) Primary School, Bury St Edmunds**

## LAVANA VS WATERHORSE

Back before humans, a monster ruled the world. He was named Lavana. He had a volcano as a head, lava around the cracks of his rocky body. The Waterhorse was sick of him so she challenged him to a battle. The battle was epic but the Waterhorse was triumphant.

Joe McColgan (11)
**Hothfield Junior School, Silsden**

## SHADOW

I came in and it was dark. No one was home, but I heard a sound coming from upstairs. I went upstairs and I tiptoed in every room. Then I saw that I missed a room so I tiptoed in. All the lights were off. Then I saw a shadow.

Sophie Dolphin (11)
**Hothfield Junior School, Silsden**

## CHATTER VILLE

One dark and noisy day, the president's wife of Chatterville set off to make sure everything was upright. As she came closer to the slimy pink glowing well, she noticed Mount Chatter upside down. She soon remembered the mad voicer was making some new voices.

Alex Waterhouse (11)
**Hothfield Junior School, Silsden**

## RUNNING

All he could do was run. The never-ending forest was awaiting him. As he entered the dense trees he heard the creature coming closer. He ran on, gasping for air until he reached a clearing. Suddenly he felt a man grasping him, pulling him to safety from the beast.

Abigail Horner (11)
**Hothfield Junior School, Silsden**

## BEN'S BRAND NEW DEN

On Sunday Ben Beck was in his brand new den, made of sticks. He suddenly heard a twig snap. He looked up. It was the cyclops. Ben ran as fast as he could towards the house. The cyclops had hold of his leg, and dragged Ben back to his den.

Callum Boocock (11)

**Hothfield Junior School, Silsden**

## THE FANO (FAR-NOO) BIRD

One magical evening a creature of unimaginable power and great strength came! Soaring like a bird of light, the giant beast accelerated through the once silent forest. Powerful beams crushed the darkness that attempted to devour the bird. What was this majestic ball of living light? The fano of course!

Neva Thomas (11)

**Hothfield Junior School, Silsden**

# THE TOMADIS

Bobobolys set off on a treacherous journey to defeat the Tomadis. Two men named Alexander and Philopolys tried to persuade Bobobolys to take a weapon but he refused every time they tried. The journey seemed agonisingly long but he got to the top. Bobobolys kicked and punched but he died.

Owen Barrett (10)
**Hothfield Junior School, Silsden**

# THE PUNKAROT

A long time ago people thought that there was not a more tasty thing than what they had, so a brave boy said, 'I know of a tastier thing than what we have: a punkarot!'
The next day they found a skeleton near to a punkarot.
Are punkarots animals?

Matthew Breare (11)
**Hothfield Junior School, Silsden**

## THE SENMUT'S TRIUMPH

The woods were dark and gloomy as Sylvie entered through a clearing of trees, looking for her dog Paws. She crept silently past an oak tree. That was the last place anyone saw her. Only the trees heard her scream in terror, as the senmut grasped its prey feeling triumphant.

Lauren Wurzal (11)

**Hothfield Junior School, Silsden**

## GOLDFISH IN THE BOG

I swim around, five seconds pass. What was I just doing? I glare out of the glass bowl. Someone's coming. Five seconds pass. How did that person get there? The person slips, the glass shatters. Five seconds pass. Why has the water gone? Water! Why am I in the toilet?

Lauren Smith (11)

**Hothfield Junior School, Silsden**

# THE AUDITION

John, an actor, got an audition for a TV show. As soon as he came back, Charlie, his friend, asked, 'How did it go?'
'It went horribly wrong! I messed up every line!' John moaned.
'Oh well, never mind,' Charlie sighed.
'Just kidding! They loved me! I got the part!'

Rachael Robinson (11)

**Hothfield Junior School, Silsden**

# CREEPY KITTY

Dom sat still. He was sure he heard the stairs creak. He decided to check to see if anybody was actually coming in to kill him. But before he could move the silent predator pounced onto its prey. The predator growled loudly. 'Miaow!'
'Argh!' Dom shouted, 'oh Kitty, it's you.'

Billy Cubitt (11)

**Hothfield Junior School, Silsden**

## REVENGE

The day had come when Zico would travel to the land of the wizards to get his revenge on Merdena. A year ago Merdena defeated him so Zico retreated. It didn't take long for him to find Merdena. Zico pulled out his sword and thrust it into Merdena's heart.

Samuel Jackson (11)

**Hothfield Junior School, Silsden**

## THE OLD WORLD AND THE SAPTIOR

It was back when the world was new. When the saptior lived. He travelled the land eating all the people. One day a girl went to kill the saptior. She went to his cave. The saptior ran out. She pulled out her sword. *Swoop.* She'd killed the saptior. Peace again.

Lucy Smith (11)

**Hothfield Junior School, Silsden**

## THE CASE

'It's the day. Amy get up, get ready, get dressed, you're going to be late for the race!' my mum shouted. So I got dressed and went.
One of the coaches shouted, 'Go!'
I ran. I got close to the finish. I ran through the red ribbon then ...
'Winner!'

Alicia Biggs (11)
**Hothfield Junior School, Silsden**

## THE POND OF ETERNAL LIFE

There was a man named James. One day he set off on a journey to discover the pool of eternal life. He had to climb mountains and camp in cold weather. He found the water and drank. On his way back from the water, a lion appeared. James sliced it!

Hannah Kayley (11)
**Hothfield Junior School, Silsden**

## THE GINGERBREAD MAN

One day in a land far away a little man was sprinting along a round path. All of a sudden he tripped and fell. His brown tasty biscuit leg fell off. The little man got up crying, limping and singing. 'You can't catch me because I'm a broken gingerbread man.'

Sonnie MacFarlane (11)
**Isambard Brunel Junior School, Portsmouth**

## ESCAPE OF THE CHICKEN

The rooster called. The chickens woke up to another day of slavery with no freedom. Until little Mac lectured the chickens that they should escape and be free. With a lot of might they broke through the heavily barbed fence and ... got brutally massacred by savage, bloodthirsty foxes.

Sami Rahman (11)
**Isambard Brunel Junior School, Portsmouth**

## UNTITLED

There was a boy called Andrew. He was 16 years old. One day he went to the woods and saw a house, he wondered if he crept in the house and a doll began to follow him. He ran quickly back home to Mum. Screaming, 'Argh!'

Tabitha Myra (9)
**Langland Community School, Milton Keynes**

## UNTITLED

One sunny morning a girl named Sophie went underwater to have a little swim. Suddenly a big sparkly wave splashed on to her and she instantly turned in to a mermaid. But then she saw a rainbow fish swimming and she liked the rainbow fish so she stayed in there.

Malkia Juma (9)
**Langland Community School, Milton Keynes**

## THE DARK MISTY FOREST

One strange day a man went to sleep and woke up in a dark, scary, diabolical place. He wandered for a while. He bumped into a man but it wasn't a man, it was Grim Reaper! He ran off panicking because he'd forgotten something. Then silence, just silence ...

Joshua Holian (10)
**Linthorpe Primary School, Middlesbrough**

## THE DRAGON

I was running away on Volcano Island, and a huge fiery dragon was chasing me! It was breathing fire, trying to burn me to death! The volcano erupted ... lava and hot molten rock burst out! The dragon was gaining on me ... I was doomed. I'm now trapped ... goodbye cruel world ...

Jamal Banaras (10)
**Linthorpe Primary School, Middlesbrough**

## TERROR DREAM

I was wandering into a gloomy cave, then … noises. I looked behind and there were pale vampires with blood dripping down. Gruesome aliens and floating faces … coming closer, running into an endless cave …
'Wake up, Ben, time for school.'

Dina Al-Asadi (10)

**Linthorpe Primary School, Middlesbrough**

## ALIEN MADNESS

I was going up to scary space and I was really nervous. When I got up there I was met eye to eye with aliens, I was surrounded. There was only one thing to do, run!
Fifteen minutes later I was home, safe and sound, *alone!*

Leigha Donnelly (10)

**Linthorpe Primary School, Middlesbrough**

## THE GHOST

The knight entered the haunted castle. Noises all around. A door slammed, the floor creaked, just then the ghost jumped out! The knight slashed him. A head rolled across the floor. 'Ha-ha!' shouted the knight. He ran away before anyone could see ...
'Harry, time for tea!'

Jessica McGough (10)
**Linthorpe Primary School, Middlesbrough**

## UNTITLED

We'd been 12 days in the submarine when my crew saw a gigantic shark. It used its huge teeth and bit the submarine. It started to flood. Trish screamed. Bill told her to calm down. The water got higher and higher. The glass started to break ...

Gabriel Lee (9)
**Linthorpe Primary School, Middlesbrough**

## FAIRY GLEN

It was dark, gloomy, cold and wintry. I stormed into the cave. I know I had to stop it. But when? But how? Coming out of the cave, I flew over mountains which were near the cave. I looked for the bird. It wasn't there. But why?

Arina Hussain (10)
**Linthorpe Primary School, Middlesbrough**

## THE DEATH WAR II

Here I am. *Ping!* In a German trench, *boom!* It's scary now. *Bang!* Death's everywhere. Just yesterday Sarge died. *Zoom!* Bombers, tanks everywhere. Everyone's calling it Death War. *Bang!* But I call it Death War II. *Vroom!* We're not spotted so far oh no!

Harry Coghlan (10)
**Linthorpe Primary School, Middlesbrough**

## THE DARK CAVE

Here I am in a dark, gloomy, spider-infested cave. 'Argh!' Twisting and turning. I pull out my sword, there is nothing there. I crawl closer and closer to where the sound comes from. Then I come face to face with ...

Tom Petch (10)
**Linthorpe Primary School, Middlesbrough**

## WHERE COULD IT BE?

Indiana Jones entered the dark, gloomy, wet and bat-infested cave ... *crash!* Boulders fell down behind him, he froze. He saw a shadow. He was looking but he couldn't find it. The old crazy man said it was here, someone had taken it. Where could it be?

Robert Carter (10)
**Linthorpe Primary School, Middlesbrough**

## IT

I'm here. After 2 years of travelling through dusty, raging rapids and rocky roads, I'm here. I just need to find it. Where is it? He said it was here ... There's the stand. But where's it gone? Oh no. Two years of travelling and it's gone.

Lauren Dalton (10)
**Linthorpe Primary School, Middlesbrough**

## THE STRANDED SOLDIER

*Boom! Ratatatat!* 'Get down!' War soldiers dying all the time. Britain vs? What are those things? Are they aliens? Whatever they are they're going down. *'Argh!' Zzzz! Boom! 'Argh!'*
Later on, 'Er what happened?'
'Everybody's dead!'
The stranded soldier walked on west, then he took one step. *Rumble ...*

Saul Myer Willson-Spencer (10)
**Linthorpe Primary School, Middlesbrough**

## ADVENTURE IN THE DESERT

There she was, surrounded by the sun, the dust and the heat. She heard a sound. What was it? She was wondering what it could be in this scorching, hot desert. 'Oh no, argh!' ...

Alisha Gulbahar (10)
**Linthorpe Primary School, Middlesbrough**

## ADVENTURE IN THE DESERT

In the middle of the huge, hot and dusty desert she heard a sound. It was getting louder and louder. Then she heard footsteps coming closer and closer. She heard a scream and a bang ...

Mardia Ali (10)
**Linthorpe Primary School, Middlesbrough**

## DANGER AHEAD

Hurtling through branches and leaves I slip off a 100ft cliff. I cling to a rock, fighting for my life. Suddenly a screeching eagle comes straight at me, flying over the void. I heave myself to safety, glancing aimlessly I spot it. It's there, it's safe.

Elliott Lynch (10)
**Linthorpe Primary School, Middlesbrough**

## THE BEAST OF HERRING

In the little town of Herring a legend scatters minds. A half-man, half-bat wanders the deep, dark and soundless sewers. I know this because I was the first to experience it. It has torn a huge part out of my life. Because ... I am the beast of Herring!

Hashim Hussain (10)
**Linthorpe Primary School, Middlesbrough**

## ABBIE AND THE DEMENTOR

One spooky night Abbie was walking when she heard a scream coming from the abandoned warehouse. She ran to the warehouse to find a Dementor taking a girl's memory. Abbie screamed, 'Expelliamus.' The Dementor flew up the chimney.
The next day Abbie got given a medal for defeating the Dementor.

Laura Duncan (10)

**Linthorpe Primary School, Middlesbrough**

## WHAT!

What is it? I don't know where I am. Dad said it was here but then I saw this thing looking like a hedgehog. Then it saw me. Then I ran into a dark, gloomy, infested cave. *Bang, bang, bang.*

Tahani Owarth (10)

**Linthorpe Primary School, Middlesbrough**

# ASLEEP FOREVER, NOT ME

Michael was captured in a huge castle by the ugliest witch ever. Suddenly the bravest knight, Alex, crashed through the castle wall, rescuing Michael from being put to sleep forever. The old wizard was delighted so, in a flash, he changed them back to children to enjoy their adventures together.

Alex Geddes (10)

**Linthorpe Primary School, Middlesbrough**

# ESSAY PRIZE

Justin has won an essay competition to go on the SS Tipton Teen cruise to Hawaii. His sister Alex can't go because she has sixteen missing assignments. She finds out that there is a school on-board. But then she sinks the ship.

Joe Murphy (10)

**Linthorpe Primary School, Middlesbrough**

## TENPORTAL TOWER

Time is being crushed. Tenportal Tower is crumbling. Jerry skitters in - his destiny awaits ... There is one way. *Up!*
He arrives at the top. A T-rex is breaking the time portal. Grabbing his tail, Jerry launches him off the tower. Time is fixed. Jerry becomes an entity among legends.

James Wade-Iles (9)

**Maldon Primary School, Maldon**

## HAUNTED HOUSE

One gloomy night a nervous but brave girl walks into a house. She walks up the creaky stairs to her new room. She thinks it is haunted. Suddenly the door slams in her face. She calls for help, her mum runs up the stairs and unlocks the door.

Cassie Syder (9)

**Maldon Primary School, Maldon**

## THE CREEPY FREAKY NIGHT

Once creepy night there was a frightening castle. There was a dirty little cute girl aged 5. As she was going around she was touching timidly at the things in the castle. The little girl took the crown. The little girl got out with the magical sparkly crown.

Lucy Sapsed (9)

**Maldon Primary School, Maldon**

## THE HAUNTED MANSION

One gloomy night in a dark and misty mansion there lived a beautiful young girl named Katie. One stormy night Katie suddenly saw a bright light towering above her. She slowly and quietly tiptoed up the creaky stairs. There in front of her lay a huge puddle of bright red blood.

Grace Rutland (9)

**Maldon Primary School, Maldon**

## ALICE IN IMAGINARY WORLD!

One glittery day a girl called Alice was invited to a wedding for her aunt. She was 12 years old. She fell down a hole in a tree trunk. It was an extraordinary land. She thought it was a dream. She danced with Rat, then found a ladder. She climbed.

Mikaella McIntosh (9)
**Maldon Primary School, Maldon**

## THE TIGER WHO ESCAPED FROM THE ZOO

One day Adventure Island was packed with people, the weather was scorching hot. That day a tiger escaped from the zoo and frightened everybody away. Then it hopped on a ride and screeched, 'Yeah baby yeah!' But it really was a silly man dressed in a tiger suit.

Lauren Walker (8)
**Maldon Primary School, Maldon**

## THE PRINCESS AND THE DRAGON

On Magical Island there was a pretty princess watering her flowers. She saw a dragon. He was tired like a sleepy dog. His eyes were red like diamonds in the sky. He lifted her into the sky. Her eyes were blue like a blue cloud.

Scarlet Cadwell (9)
**Maldon Primary School, Maldon**

## LEWIS THE CHICKEN

Lewis the chicken came across a man with a black cape. Terry was an evil chicken who tried to kidnap Lewis. The cloaked man heard a noise and ran to help Lewis. Terry pulled Lewis one way and the cloaked man pulled the other, will Lewis survive the battle?

Harry Wood (9)
**Maldon Primary School, Maldon**

## THE CHICKEN

A chicken was in his pen house with his mates, they were talking about going mountaineering. One of the chickens shouted, 'Let's go mountaineering.'
The other chickens shouted, 'No way Jose.' But the other chicken set off. The chicken found a mountain that was actually a volcano.

Samuel Beattie (9)

**Maldon Primary School, Maldon**

## MELODY MERMAID'S FISHY FIASCO

Once there was a beautiful mermaid, Melody. She lived in an undersea palace with her family. Melody's sapphire tail swished around as she rode her dolphin. She giggled happily. She arrived at an empty palace. Suddenly lights flashed, her friends and family yelled, 'Surprise!'
*Wow,* Melody thought, *what a birthday*.

Milly Ball (9)

**Maldon Primary School, Maldon**

## THE UNWANTED VISITOR

It is a stormy night; I decide to venture through the moors. There's footsteps. I turn. I see it. It pounces. I fall back to the earth. He's staring at me. I stand back. A deformed figure. He's now running; a racer. I shut my eyes. My life has faded.

Rai Osborne (9)
**Maldon Primary School, Maldon**

## UNITED AT LAST

Trixie lives in a glittering glen with glowing bushes and towering trees. One beautiful day, a strange rustling noise occurrs. Is it a fox, or a bear? Trixie goes to explore, an adventure. Suddenly, something makes her jolt. She turns gradually and grins. Her brother! What a fabulous, funny surprise!

Eloise Tomkins (9)
**Maldon Primary School, Maldon**

## THE HOUSE OF THE DEAD

Tom finds a spooky haunted house with dead bodies, voices, huge cobwebs and a thousand graveyards. He knocks the gigantic knocker and spiders come out. Dead bodies hang. A giant spider grabs his leg viciously. He luckily escapes through an open window. Tom sprints to the graveyards desperately to hide.

Sam Tregidgo (9)
**Maldon Primary School, Maldon**

## THE STRANGE SOUNDS!

Rebecca is in a beautiful forest lit by moonlight. She hears the patter of wet feet. The sound gets louder, an enormous elephant stomping. She starts to shake. A huge, cuddly dog leaps out. It is a fluffy dog. Rebecca keeps the lovely dog as a guard and loves him.

Martha Thomas (9)
**Maldon Primary School, Maldon**

# THE INVASION

The frightened man zoomed into a rocky cave, a fast racing car. A blue ship came down, he was beaten up! Inside robots attacked him. In anger he pressed a button. (*Bang!*) He slipped off the ship. He landed on concrete. He died knowing he bombed up their blue ship.

Alex Bridgman (9)
**Maldon Primary School, Maldon**

# THE UNEXPECTED ADVENTURE

Georgina and her kind, fluffy dog are on the mystical moors when they see some men carrying stolen possessions. So they sprint to the police and show them the way. The men get captured so she walks home to tell her parents her strange adventure. She's glad to be home.

Rachael Sullivan (9)
**Maldon Primary School, Maldon**

## GHOST MURDER

In a freaky wood there's a girl called Lizzy. She hears a branch crack. She spots a ghost. Lizzy picks up her 'How To Murder Ghosts' book. It reads that ghosts dislike water so she gets out her water bottle and hurls it at the ghost until he suddenly disappears.

Erin Corby (9)
**Maldon Primary School, Maldon**

## THE GRAVEYARD SPIDER

As she ran across the graveyard, a huge spider she spotted sitting on its web, chewing a fly's guts. Then it ran across the side. Was it the spider what caused that shadow? In no time I got my razorblade, silver sword out. I stabbed it. Eventually it was dead!

Chloe Williams (8)
**Maldon Primary School, Maldon**

## LUCY'S WEIRD DAY

Lucy spotted a pitch black ghostly house and wanted to enter. She tiptoed in nervously. After that, Lucy heard a noise. It came from the door. She sidled to the door and spotted a Minotaur. A few minutes later, the Minotaur was on the floor bleeding. Lucy never went back.

Harriet Reeve (9)

**Maldon Primary School, Maldon**

## ROMANCE IS DEAD

It was Valentine's Day. The man's wife was sitting sadly, in the corner crying. The lady was having a cup of tea. This woman was tired. She heard a mutter from the kitchen. The window slammed. The trees swayed, slowly. Timidly she tiptoed into the kitchen like a mouse, surprise!

Katie Maxwell (9)

**Maldon Primary School, Maldon**

## THE PRETEND GHOST

In a spooky, dark, scary street, a ghost jumped out of an alley on some people. The people tried fighting back at him. The ghost was too fast for them and ran away. The people whipped his costume off and then they found out that it was their friend Fred!

Lewis Bridge (9)
**Maldon Primary School, Maldon**

## THE MONSTER ATTACK

It was a dark spooky night. Lights were flickering. We saw a repulsive monster, we ran but Sarah tripped. The monster yanked her up and locked her in a cage. Dad had to save Sarah. Into the cave. He picked Sarah up and ran.
Two weeks later they moved house.

Kieran Wenlock (9)
**Maldon Primary School, Maldon**

## ALIEN ATTACK

In an old creepy churchyard aliens hide in the bush. The aliens throw a ball at me and it shoots out an electric beam. I feel like I am changing, my body turns pea green and my face turns blue and I grow horns and tusks. I am an alien.

Lewis Hawes (8)
**Maldon Primary School, Maldon**

## THE GHOSTLY FOREST

In the gloomy forest, a whisper. They are coming! As a gust of wind hit, the girl was chilly. While the wind curled and swirled, two eyes appeared. The girl knew something terrible was up. 'Hello little girl. Are you good or bad?'
Scared she said, 'I'm good,' while shivering.

Connor Healey (9)
**Maldon Primary School, Maldon**

## MIDNIGHT FINDS A NEW OWNER

Midnight is a puppy. He gets lost. He is staying in a street. Midnight hears noises, hears someone coming. The person finds him, takes him to the vets so he can be checked over. The vet finds out that he's a stray. He finds an owner. He loves his family.

Alexandra Hember (9)
**Maldon Primary School, Maldon**

## DINOSAUR MURDER ON SUNDAY NIGHT

In a deadly, haunted mansion Alex entered. There were spooky ghosts and black-fanged spiders. 'What was that smash outside?' screamed Alex, shaking nervously, like machines rattling. She rushed outside to see what it was. 'A dinosaur! Help!' They fought and Alex got hurt badly. 'Please help me! Someone help!'

Emily Swinger (9)
**Maldon Primary School, Maldon**

## WINGS TURNS TO SLEEP

One twinkling day, Rose bought a dog. His name was Buster. Rose sat patiently on a luscious flower and got wings.
Later, Rose found Buster was unwell so she took him to the vets. On the way, Rose got tired so she calmly sat on another flower. Buster slept forever.

Isobel Frost (9)
**Maldon Primary School, Maldon**

## BORED

Lily was bored of her DS. She couldn't get to the toadstool temple. A noise came from her DS. It was saying, 'Lily.' Someone called her then she seemed to see her name everywhere, on the walls, even on the bed. She checked her DS screen, but was never found.

Ashlea Lacey (10)
**Maldon Primary School, Maldon**

## THE DRAGON

Octavia ran away from the giant dragon which followed her. She ran to Fairy Glen which was where she lived but the door was locked, she couldn't get in. She ran to her treehouse. She climbed the steps but found she was looking into the eyes of the giant dragon.

Charlotte Martin (9)
**Maldon Primary School, Maldon**

## THE WHALE AND HIS WORLD

A graceful whale jumped out of the water, his glistening skin shone. He took me under, I held his fin as he took me deeper to his world. Ruined; I couldn't bear it. I asked to go up, he took me to the surface. He whispered, 'Help my world, please.'

Tianna Morfett (10)
**Maldon Primary School, Maldon**

## WONDER PICTURE

Max was an artist. Exploring the woods, he began to draw a beautiful hidden lake. It looked real, moss on the rocks and sparkles on the water. He blinked, his picture came to life, he dived into the water and saw fish never seen before, he wished to stay forever.

Giovanni Bird (10)
**Maldon Primary School, Maldon**

## BLACK TEARS

When Lilly cried, her tears were black. She told her parents, they laughed, called her silly. She threw the tears at her parents, they melted. She cried and cried, one of her tears fell on her chest her heart melted. She's still around but now she can't cry … as much.

Roni-Anne Winch (10)
**Maldon Primary School, Maldon**

## THE SPOOKY ALIEN GHOSTS

I was sad because the spooky ghost came around me all the time. A ghost was talking to me. I was coming down the stairs and I felt ghosts were being nice now. I ran with them to the spaceship and played with them. 'Take me with you!' I said.

Kyle Kirby (9)

**Maldon Primary School, Maldon**

## THE TIGER FINDS A GIRLFRIEND

The little tiger was born in its warm cosy cave. Then he grew up to hunt his own food, he got to his new home. He wanted a beautiful girlfriend because he needed to have babies. He found a pregnant tigress and then he had a baby just like him!

Joshua Bailey (8)

**Maldon Primary School, Maldon**

# THE LETTER

Ashley and Jake found some mysterious letters. Jake opened the letter there were words missing, the envelope in the corner said *look in your garden.* They found another envelope, inside there was another letter, it has the missing words in it and they said *you are going to die today.*

Ashley Knight (9)

**Maldon Primary School, Maldon**

# CINDERELLA

Cinderella wanted to go to the ball but her wicked stepsisters wouldn't let her go. She started to cry as the stepsisters disappeared into the darkness. *Boom!* It was her fairy godmother. 'You will go to the ball to meet the prince,' said her fairy godmother.

Lucy Pickard (9)

**North Stainley CE Primary School, Ripon**

## THE CASTLE OF DOOM!

John was on his holidays in Scotland. One day he saw a strange old person lumber in to a dark old castle ...
An hour later the old man had not come out. John was baffled. Then he went in and found out that it was a hotel.

Sam Mansfield (9)
**North Stainley CE Primary School, Ripon**

## UNTITLED

Beth awoke, had she heard something or was it a dream? She crept down the stairs terrified, nervous of what she might find. She turned the stiff handle. She entered the room. Suddenly a dark figure pounced on her. Luckily it was only the cat messing around.

Laura Donaldson (9)
**North Stainley CE Primary School, Ripon**

# THE THREE LITTLE CATS AND THE BIG BAD MOUSE

One day three little cats were snuggling in front of the fire. Suddenly a big shadow crowded over them. It was the thing they were most scared of. It was ... the big bad mouse. They made a big mousetrap. Then he was never seen again.

Phoebe Dawber (10)

**North Stainley CE Primary School, Ripon**

# IT WAS ONLY A DREAM

Rain was dripping down my neck, I ran through the deserted streets. A bloodcurdling figure on my trail, a stench of rotting flesh ... It was about to strike. A pain in my side, I fell ... and I ended up on my bedroom floor. It was only a dream.

Cameron O'Donnell (11)

**North Stainley CE Primary School, Ripon**

## CINDERELLA

Cinderella sat and cried. 'I cannot go to the ball,' she sobbed. 'I will never get a chance to meet the prince,' she said as she watched the two stepsisters go to the ball.

*Boom!* Her fairy godmother appeared, 'You will go to the ball!'

Emma Jones (9)

**North Stainley CE Primary School, Ripon**

## ONE SCARY NIGHT

I had just come home from gym. I said to myself, 'I'm sure she said five.'

I knocked once, there was no answer. I knocked again, no reply. I walked in through the creaky door, I tiptoed through. There were some mysterious noises. Ahhh! I was never seen again!

Clara Hart (11)

**Oundle & King's Cliffe Middle School, Oundle**

## THE MONSTER

Jim and Guss were running through the forest but then they saw something, it was a monster. It was coming closer, 'Run!' shouted Jim.
'It's getting closer!' shouted Guss. 'Argh!' they both shouted. The monster stopped, they stopped, it took its face off, it was Pete. 'Hey, it's Pete.'

George Sloggett (11)

**Oundle & King's Cliffe Middle School, Oundle**

## UNTITLED

I wasn't scared. Then before I knew it, I was off running. My legs were carrying me so fast, they felt out of control. I was neck and neck with the other girl. Then I felt a rush. One metre away. I felt hard ground, I fell over!

Rosie Fisher (11)

**Oundle & King's Cliffe Middle School, Oundle**

## DARKNESS

Dave came home, he opened the door, nobody was home. He heard a creak from upstairs. He went upstairs and two red eyes glared right at him inside a pitch black room. He took three steps back, but then it came out from the darkness ...

William Baker (11)
**Oundle & King's Cliffe Middle School, Oundle**

## THE MYSTERY

Rebecca, Jordan, Nicole and Jay were playing. They were supposed to be back by 7.00. It was now 10.30. They were out playing near the river and saw two men walk past. The next minute there was a big, loud *bang!* Then it was silent. They were never seen again.

Rebecca White (11)
**Oundle & King's Cliffe Middle School, Oundle**

# DOOMSDAY

Red, red, red, red, red, out! The starting lights had gone we were racing down the straight towards Stowe turn one, Hamilton in the lead, Jenson Button in second and Webber in third. Webber was being closely followed by Alonso. Alonso went to overtake he edged Webber and flipped over.

Gabriel Smithson (11)
**Oundle & King's Cliffe Middle School, Oundle**

# THE MAN RIDING A UNICORN

One day I was walking home from school, I saw a man riding a unicorn; I was amazed, I must be dreaming. So I pinched myself. I didn't wake up. I must be awake. The man on the unicorn saw me and swooped down and offered me a ride home.

Kate Watson (11)
**Oundle & King's Cliffe Middle School, Oundle**

## MY MUM'S A CLOWN!

Well, I always thought she had no sense of humour. But on Sunday nights she'd go out and come back on an elephant, how weird is that?

Dylan Walsh (10)
**Oundle & King's Cliffe Middle School, Oundle**

## THE SHOW

The curtains opened. My heart thumped. I started to play my piece. The others joined in. We finished. The audience clapped. The curtains closed. Everyone sighed a sigh of relief. It went better than I thought. We went back on for a bow. Phew, the show was over at last.

Anna Hilbert (11)
**Oundle & King's Cliffe Middle School, Oundle**

## THE LANDSCAPE

Me and my friend were playing tig, my friend was it, I looked back to see but I couldn't, looking forward I saw monstrous grey mountains, sky blue water, turquoise blue waterfalls and the griffin. I thought I was dreaming. *Bang!* My friend bumped me off the sloped cliff's edge.

Reece Lendrum (11)
**Oundle & King's Cliffe Middle School, Oundle**

## INDIANA BONES

One day Indiana Bones swung on a vine and fell off because he had no muscles! He never goes to the gym. He found a parachute just in time. He survived! 'Yip -' *Bang!* Skeleton King shot him!

Thomas Chesterman (9)
**Oundle & King's Cliffe Middle School, Oundle**

## THE HAUNTED CHURCH

Georgia and Katy went into the church freezing chills went down their spines. They saw the ghost of the last vicar that died a week ago and they just stood there rooted to the spot. They didn't know what to do, they were scared stiff. They were so scared.

Caitlin Laughton (11)
**Oundle & King's Cliffe Middle School, Oundle**

## PETRIFIED PATRICK

It was terrible, my name is Patrick and I had been blinded a couple of years ago. What happened was: I was on a climbing frame, and these two bullies pushed me off. That was it, I was blinded forever.

Craig Retchless (10)
**Oundle & King's Cliffe Middle School, Oundle**

## UNTITLED

Peter Pinch was known for his fabulous pancake making skills. They sizzled and fizzled and plopped in the pan with a flip and a flop whist he tried not to drop. One day he ran out of lemon and they tasted like snake's venom. Then his shop never opened again.

Katy Measures (11)

**Oundle & King's Cliffe Middle School, Oundle**

## MY BEST FRIEND

I had a best friend who thought he was the best, I proved him wrong by doing a test, I got all the answers by saying a rhyme, then I realised he did a crime. Now I feel really guilty by being mean.

Ella Watson (10)

**Oundle & King's Cliffe Middle School, Oundle**

## HELP ME!

One day I heard a fairy speaking saying, 'Help, save me I'm stuck.'
So I went to search for the fairy. I found her under a toadstool, it was raining. I saved her and kept her in a box forgetting to feed her, and she was never seen again.

Savannah Streather (10)

**Oundle & King's Cliffe Middle School, Oundle**

## GHOSTLY GOING ON

There was a creak in the boards downstairs. I saw its teeth were ripping my dog. I jumped like Tarzan and swung on the lights. Ahhh, I wrestled the monster and got my puppies back.

Dylan Kilford (10)

**Oundle & King's Cliffe Middle School, Oundle**

## A DISAPPOINTING DAY

*Trit trot,* along I rode.
They're going to kill you, I was told.
'What?' I said.
'I'm going to meet them for ale and bread.'
I got to the inn and they shot me.
I fell. Ouch, my knee.
They laughed. 'Whatever,' I replied.
At least I had not cried.

Alice Smith (10)
**Oundle & King's Cliffe Middle School, Oundle**

## HOW PONIES AND HORSES CAME TO EARTH

With a pow and a bang from the human. Then a ting and a tang from the church bells. Then *kaboom.* There it was, the pony and the horse!

Celeste McAughtrie (10)
**Oundle & King's Cliffe Middle School, Oundle**

## CHILLI PEPPER CHARLIE TO A LEGEND IN THE WORLD

'Chilli' Charlie had had all the chillies in the *world!* Now he was having the choppillili chilli! The hottest chilli! As he was having it, he went red and ... *exploded!* There will never be a person more into chillies than Chilli Pepper Legend Charlie.

James Ray (10)

**Oundle & King's Cliffe Middle School, Oundle**

## JIMMY

There once was a boy called Jimmy, he had a best friend called Timmy, they watched TV all night, it was a pretty good sight, but that is because the TV is HD.

Alex Wilkinson (10)

**Oundle & King's Cliffe Middle School, Oundle**

## MY HEADTEACHER IS EVIL

My headteacher is evil. It all started when I was sent into her office. Her door was open a crack. I looked through. I could not believe my eyes. Her room was lit purple and when she turned around her eyes were red. I know she is evil now.

Ellie Sanders (10)

**Oundle & King's Cliffe Middle School, Oundle**

## FORENSIC!

One day the police came to our school, they called for me. I became worried. They started to talk about a discovery of a body found near the First Drift. I was taken there. But oh! All they wanted me for was to help them discover the mystery!

Jade Cunnington (10)

**Oundle & King's Cliffe Middle School, Oundle**

## NAUGHTY GIRL!

Katy Measures is a naughty girl who likes to pick her nose. She loves her gerbils so much she makes them little clothes. She took her gerbils to school one day when the gerbils decided to bite her poor old teacher who ran into the corridor in fright.

Holly Clancy (11)
**Oundle & King's Cliffe Middle School, Oundle**

## THE CAVE

I tripped over stones, the cave was dark, I heard noises, there was something on my shoe, I screamed. It was a rat. Suddenly I stepped in a hole, I was stuck, I shivered, *boom! Step! Step! Creak!* There was something at the back of the cave, I blacked out.

Natasha Mason (10)
**Oundle & King's Cliffe Middle School, Oundle**

## HELP!

I was hanging onto the vine and beneath me was a colossal crocodile. My hands were sweating and I was slipping down towards the beast. Then he burped and knocked me off the vine, into his huge mouth. The next thing I realised was that the beast's teeth pierced me!

Emily Thomas-Fahy (10)

**Oundle & King's Cliffe Middle School, Oundle**

## HAPPY BIRTHDAY!

It was my birthday, I opened the door to my classroom, they were hiding behind their chairs. I had just been to the doctors. Suddenly they jumped out and said, 'Happy birthday.' I was so embarrassed.

Sophia Ginns (10)

**Oundle & King's Cliffe Middle School, Oundle**

## THE GOAL

I put the ball down for a penalty. I took a run up, and booted it with power. Everyone watched it fly through the air. Then it went in the goal, and my heart in my soul was saying yes I scored a goal.

Hannah Sayer (10)

**Oundle & King's Cliffe Middle School, Oundle**

## THE ELEPHANT ROCK

One early morning the unfortunate people were gathering crabs and winkles from the lonely rock pools scattered across the deserted beach. The Elephant Rock loomed ominously in the background. A small boat sailed slowly by while the silent lighthouse looked on. Suddenly peace was shattered, the elephant came to life . . .

Owen McCabe

**Owton Manor Primary School, Hartlepool**

# THE LOOMING ATMOSPHERE

As the cheerless sky gave way, the Elephant Rock loomed in the background and the unfortunate people savaged their way into the water, collecting seafood. A sailboat watched on. In the distance a lighthouse stood silently. Suddenly, Mam shouted, 'Lights out, half-nine, time for bed - no time to read.'

Emily Hordijk (11)
**Owton Manor Primary School, Hartlepool**

# UNTITLED

One foggy morning lots of poor people went onto the beach as the tide went out. There were lots of crabs out on the beach for the poor people to collect. Once collected they needed to be delivered to the rich people. The poor would go hungry again.

Shaun Hadfield (11)
**Owton Manor Primary School, Hartlepool**

## THE SAILOR TO BE!

In 1998, a (sailor to be) was born. Eleven years later ...
'Mum, I feel a bit sick, can you drop down the anchor?'
'No, you'll get used to it,' shouted Mum.
The waves crept on-board and grabbed Leigh by the ankle. 'Help me!'
Would Leigh survive? What would happen?

Leigh Turner (11)

**Owton Manor Primary School, Hartlepool**

## THE VICTORIAN SHIPWRECK

It was 1852, a ship was sailing to Hartlepool. The captain became confused by thick blankets of fog. Due to this, he lost his sight of the bay and crashed into rocks. The wood from the ship scattered upon the shore. People gathered, collected wood, they would survive the winter.

Danika Cass (11)

**Owton Manor Primary School, Hartlepool**

## THE ROCK POOL

One early morning poor people came out of their houses to collect crabs from the rock pool. While they were collecting crabs a big elephant stood watching them. A ship sailed in the distance. Suddenly Mum shouted, 'Tea's ready, turn off the TV!'

Callum Sudron (11)

**Owton Manor Primary School, Hartlepool**

## UNTITLED

Many years ago, in the 1950s, wood spread on the cool grey sand of Hartlepool beach. The ship, Otaa, left the wood stranded after it capsized and sunk into the murky waters below. Thousands of poor people found and collected the wood. This would keep them warm throughout winter.

Alexandra Marshall (11)

**Owton Manor Primary School, Hartlepool**

## THE FISHERMEN

While the wind swept through the air, the fishermen prepared for a fishing trip at sea. As they were setting sail, the smoky fog spread through the atmosphere. The dog started to bark while the bells rang loudly in the distance. What would be the fate of the men?

Jay Precious (10)

**Owton Manor Primary School, Hartlepool**

## THE MYSTERY THAT DESTROYED THE PEOPLE

The sea was smooth as silk while the church loomed ominously in the background. Two fishermen prepared for a day of graft upon the dark water; the old dog glared at his reflection in the water. Suddenly a great wave swept into the bay and destroyed the peace.

Brandon Moran (11)

**Owton Manor Primary School, Hartlepool**

## A RACE AROUND THE WORLD

One bright sunny morning sailors raced their sailing boats around the world. The sailors battled against the rough, wild sea. While fighting the sea, some of the sailors got hurt in the fight. The crowds cheered as the boats rounded the point. They made it safely home.

Jack Emery (11)
**Owton Manor Primary School, Hartlepool**

## ALL ABOARD!

As the black clouds zoomed around the eerie boats, the pirates attempted to attack the navy's ship. They jumped over onto the ship and successfully landed on deck. The clouds started to clear as they captured the ship. They then left their boats as food for the hungry, obnoxious sea.

Chloe Hall (11)
**Owton Manor Primary School, Hartlepool**

## THE BATTLE

As the scary black clouds closed in on the sun, pirates attacked a helpless naval ship. Victory at last. They left the old battered pirate ship to sit peacefully on the seabed. As the new ship sailed away, its pirate flag held high in the warm, breezy, calm air.

Lauren Tucker (11)
**Owton Manor Primary School, Hartlepool**

## THE SINKING SHIPS

The sky turned black as coal and the waves went crazy; while sailors blew the horn to warn everyone that the ship was sinking. Panic set in. They grabbed the food and water so they could survive. But it was too late. Suddenly there were gone. Food for the ocean!

Bethany Smedley (11)
**Owton Manor Primary School, Hartlepool**

# THE CRASH AT THE SIDE OF THE SHIP

As the black clouds surrounded the ship, the sea became wilder and wilder. The waves crashed against the rocks. The ship was moving at a very fast speed. Then suddenly, he heard a bang coming from the side of the ship …
'Ben get off your silly game,' said his mum.

Liana Cass (11)

**Owton Manor Primary School, Hartlepool**

# UNTITLED

The enraged sea slaughtered the ship with walls of water. A stunned crew fought fearlessly for their lives, as one by one, wooden beams collapsed before their eyes. Bodies became lifeless toys for the rough waves … but suddenly … 'How many time have you watched that movie?' Mum shouted …

Hollie Walker (11)

**Owton Manor Primary School, Hartlepool**

## UNTITLED

The furious waves smashed against the innocent boat which held a frightened crew. Jack, the ship's captain, was slammed against the wall as he tried to turn the ship away from the whirlpool. Suddenly Mum shouted, 'Connor get off the Xbox for once in your life.'
'But Mum!'

Connor Vasey (11)

**Owton Manor Primary School, Hartlepool**

## A WEIRD DAY

When Jasmin woke up, she was in a very big spaceship! 'Wing wong,' said a voice. A greeny sloppy thing ganged up on her shoulder. The tiny creature made her quiver and feel ill. Soon the alien disappeared by magic!

Humairaa Bobat (9)

**St Andrew's CE Primary School, Bolton**

## IN OUTER SPACE

An alien called Joe came from Mars. He went to Pluto in a spaceship and flew there. It took forty minutes to get there. He had an extremely noisy party with games. A monster came, but Joe tackled him with a head of a dragon with very sharp ears.

Isaac Randle (8)

**St Andrew's CE Primary School, Bolton**

## THE ALIEN FROM MARS

On Saturday, from the stars, came an alien! It was destroying the land of England so a group of men fought the alien for a long time because it was really powerful. But the alien was a robot so no wonder he won all battles! The English were defeated.

Kian Patel (8)

**St Andrew's CE Primary School, Bolton**

## MADACCA'S DAY OUT AT THE TRAFFORD CENTRE

One day a mythical creature called Madacca went to the Trafford Centre for a new bike. There was only a bike made of stone. So she used her snake hair powers to de-stone the bike and she rode her new bike home. 'Wee,' she said.

Regan Brown (8)
**St Andrew's CE Primary School, Bolton**

## MEDUSA

Once there were two girls called Rose and Kate. They found a cave on the beach but in the cave there was Medusa. 'Arggh! Wha - Oh!'
'Now your turn.' Then Kate got a bin top and she zapped Medusa's head. 'Waa!'
'Hooray, hooray!' they cheered.

Harriet Slamin (7)
**St Andrew's CE Primary School, Bolton**

## BEACH HOLIDAY

When I came home there lay suitcases. I said to my mum, 'What's going on?'
'Oh,' she said in a suspicious voice. 'We're going on holiday in two minutes. We're getting picked up by your Uncle Stan.' We got on the plane ...

Matthew Taylor (7)
**St Andrew's CE Primary School, Bolton**

## FRIENDS AND MEDUSA

The friends went exploring in rocky dark caves. They climbed up and down. They went into a dark cave and saw scary Medusa. They all ran away without getting turned into stone, arriving home safe and sound. They were soon in bed all snuggled, gently hugging their teddies.

Hemani Varsani (8)
**St Andrew's CE Primary School, Bolton**

## FRIENDS IN THE CAVE

One day me and my friends were walking. We went past a cave. We went in. In the cave we saw bats flying around. The bats went past. We fell down the hole. When we got up, my friends saw a treasure box. We opened it and found some jewellery.

Siya Patel (8)
**St Andrew's CE Primary School, Bolton**

## TANNED BEACH HOLIDAY

One day we went out and when we came back our mums said we were going on holiday. We were going to Florida. On the first day we went to the beach. It was so beautiful, there was cola and lollies.

Eleanor Bancks (8)
**St Andrew's CE Primary School, Bolton**

## A TRIP TO FLORIDA

One day my mum was packing but she wouldn't tell me where I was going. I was so excited. A taxi took me to the airport so I finally noticed that we were going to Florida. When we got there I quickly dived straight into the massive swimming pool.

Erin Crompton (8)
**St Andrew's CE Primary School, Bolton**

## GHOST OF FEAR

Tom ran down the slippy rocky road when suddenly a ghost dropped out of the window. The ghost scared Tom to death, it made him jump. 'Do you want a ride in my new car?'

'Of course! Where are we going?'

'We're going to the shop to get some food.'

Joe Town (8)
**St Andrew's CE Primary School, Bolton**

## SPOOKY SAM

Sam went to the park. He saw a green gooey thing. It said, 'Hello, can I come on a ride?' Sam ran back home as fast as he could.
His mum said, 'Don't be silly, it was Dad.'
'He's coming now,' Sam laughed and they lived happily ever after.

Devina Jadwa (8)

**St Andrew's CE Primary School, Bolton**

## GONG OUT TO FIGHT THE SAXONS

Mysterious smoke fills the air. Captain Bloodaxe: ginger-beaded, bold. Dark bodies rot on the rocky ground. Suddenly he hears deafening chanting. A shiver rolls down his spine. He feels lonely and thinks he will die, but his army is going to win. Remains of dried blood cover the sword.

Grace Redfern (8)

**St Andrew's CE Primary School, Bolton**

## THE MYSTERIOUS CHANGE FROM A DOG

One day Maisy was coming home from school, she had been wanting a dog, so she went to the pet shop. She went in, then she chose the dog. But, when the dog got outside the dog turned into a hairy monster! The hairy monster chased Maisy to a cave.

Keeley Orrell (8)
**St Andrew's CE Primary School, Bolton**

## AMBER'S BIRTHDAY

It was Amber's birthday. She woke up and went to the mirror. When she looked in she saw big green eyes behind her. She ran outside and just as she ran up the road and back again, she found pets outside her door. 'Thanks Mum,' she said, excitedly.

Amber Williams (8)
**St Andrew's CE Primary School, Bolton**

## OUTER SPACE

One day I was going to space. I went in a rocket with an alien. First we went to Mars then we went to Jupiter. Then we went to the moon and we played lots of games. Then we got tired and I went back home.

Daniel Sutton (8)

**St Andrew's CE Primary School, Bolton**

## BUSTER THE BEE

Buster was a very bossy boots, he wanted to be nice but he didn't know how. He kept training but he couldn't do it. One day he trained so well he became nice. Then he gathered everybody for a party. It was the best party ever!

Drvangi Kansara (8)

**St Andrew's CE Primary School, Bolton**

## A HOLIDAY IN AUSTRALIA

Danielle and I came home from school. My mum and dad said, 'We have packed for our holiday.'
I said, 'Where are we going?'
'Australia.' I was so happy. My friends were upset because I might live there.

Grace Edwards (8)

**St Andrew's CE Primary School, Bolton**

## THE HALLOWEEN SURPRISE

It was Halloween Night. The floors were creaking, the door was knocking. There was the smell of sweets in the air. I could not sleep, on the wall just next to my bedroom was a Halloween vampire and hung in my bedroom was a glow in the dark skeleton ... 'Argh!'

Ciara Smith-Hay (10)

**St Hilda's CE VC Primary School, Ampleforth**

## THE MURDER OF ARTHUR

Arthur was a boy in our class but naughty David pulled Arthur to pieces.
Years later, we found Arthur in the cupboard in our class. He was in bits. We put him back together carefully. He strangled David, now there are two skeletons in our class. Bye Arthur and David!

Matthew Lathlean (10)

**St Hilda's CE VC Primary School, Ampleforth**

## A DARK NIGHT

One dark night I walked down the pebbly road when I saw an old, dilapidated, rotten and spooky house. I slowly plucked up the courage to open the door. Then I slowly opened it and took a step in. The floorboards creaked then the door slammed shut - it locked.

Megan Mason (11)

**St Mary's RC (VA) Primary School, Stanley**

## FACE OF THE RIDE

Jonny was sitting on a 400-year-old merry-go-round. He was bored until it started. It was going at an amazing speed of 5,000mph! Jonny's feet started to slip ... *Splat!* That's all that's left of poor little Jonny. Now to this day little Jonny haunts this ride.

Samuel Sterling (11)

**St Mary's RC (VA) Primary School, Stanley**

## IDA'S STARRY NIGHT

Ida looked up at the gloomy sky, it was filled with black clouds that covered the bright shimmering stars. Her eyes were heavy and she began to fall asleep. Ida walked to her house, it was past her bedtime. Suddenly a disc flew over her head. What was it ... ?

Chloe Johnson (10)

**St Mary's RC (VA) Primary School, Stanley**

## THE BOX

It sits in the corner, silent all day but as night comes the silence fades away. Screaming, shouting, rattling around, it springs to my mind, what was that sound? As I walk towards it, the silence stops. I lift the lid. There's nothing inside. But what was that sound?

Louis Wood (10)

**Snaith Primary School, Snaith**

## THE HAUNTED SCHOOL

It was a dark night. The school children had gone home and the ghost and the vampire and everyone else had woken up. They threw things around like computers and white boards and everything else. They wrecked the place. Did anyone want to go to this school again?

Thomas Littlewood (10)

**Snaith Primary School, Snaith**

## ENCIRCLED

Walking down the sandy steps, Lily carried her lilo. She placed it in the glistening blue sea. Lying down on her lilo, she floated into deeper water. Lily was alarmed by a sudden jolt from underneath her. She sat up to find she was encircled. Would she ever get out?

Olivia Denton (10)
**Snaith Primary School, Snaith**

## THE HAUNTED HOOVER

Screaming. Bleeding as we walked through the street. Tanisha and I saw the haunted Hoover. I shouted, 'Help! Help!' because the Hoover was coming towards us. I was scared to death. The Hoover was right in front of us and then I saw it had my initials on it. How?

Olivia Robinson (10)
**Snaith Primary School, Snaith**

## THE LOCKED ROOM

I ran into my room as fast as my legs would run. It was silent. Then I heard a key turn in the keyhole. I peeped through and saw a beady red eye. I screamed with terror. Quickly I crept under my bed as the creaky old door slowly opened ...

Shannon Stewart (10)
**Snaith Primary School, Snaith**

## THE LOCKED ROOM

I was stuck. The door slammed shut, the bolt locked. The cold room smelt fishy. *Crash!* A vase fell. I screamed. This room was alive. I wanted to get out of here, so I pulled at the bolt. It stayed locked. Would I ever get out?

Niamh Slack (10)
**Snaith Primary School, Snaith**

# FRIDAY THE 13TH

The wicked night of Friday the 13th came to life as the creepy floorboards rattled in the winter breeze. I stood still in the rusty house upon the rocks. I screamed, I shouted, 'Help.' ... Locked! The door slammed, curtains blowing in thin air. Would I ever get out of here?

Bethany Davenport (10)
**Snaith Primary School, Snaith**

# JOURNEY TO THE UNKNOWN

*Crash!* My enormous time machine crashed into an unknown world. Suddenly a voice screamed out. 'Welcome to the Jurassic period!'
Carefully I crept out of my wrecked machine. It was destroyed. Then a terrified iguanadon dashed past and a tyrannosaurus stormed out of the trees. Suddenly it turned on me!

Abigail Broughton (8)
**Snaith Primary School, Snaith**

## THE HUGE ROAR

We stormed through the thick jungle leaves. There were huge colossal piles of mud. *Squelch - splosh!* Quietly we walked through. 'Argh!' A giant tiger immediately passed us, chasing its prey. Quietly but quickly we ran back through the gooey mud, back through the thick leaves and to our destination.

Yasmin Redman (8)

**Snaith Primary School, Snaith**

## MONSTER MAYHEM (A STORY TOLD BY PERCY JACKSON)

Just playing. Suddenly a huge minotaur burst through the wall! In amazement I knew that the energy sword that the old man gave me was for a dangerous reason. I sprinted to my room, slashing at this extraordinary beast. Finally, its head was off! 'That's my life! I've done it!'

Henry Stobbs (8)

**Snaith Primary School, Snaith**

## THE WD400,000 DILEMMA!

'Argh!' The lank mad scientist was gaining on me. If he hadn't caught me I wouldn't have powered up the WD400,000 (or world destroyer) 'You will never survive the fumes of toxic gas!' squealed the psychotic man, flicking a red switch ... Would I survive this meddling man and get home?

Eleanor White (9)
**Snaith Primary School, Snaith**

## MAGICAL MERMAID

'Argh!' Molly screeched. Suddenly she fell from her beautiful, pretty, glamorous rock. 'Where am I?' she asked herself.
Someone answered in a deep gloomy voice, 'You're under the sea in a shipwreck.' Who or what was behind that horrible sound? I wondered to myself. It was a shark!

Hannah Knight (8)
**Snaith Primary School, Snaith**

## MY PIRATE SHIP HAS CAPSIZED

Sleeping soundly on my floating home, a pirate ship, nothing could go wrong. Our boat would never capsize. Hours later the waves got rough, as rough as they could get. Rocking side to side, we astonishingly almost capsized. Phew! 'Help! No!' I cried.
We had scarily capsized. Would I survive?

Hannah Harrison (8)

**Snaith Primary School, Snaith**

## THE ADVENTURE

When I heard my name get called out to jump out of the helicopter, I was shaking with fear. When I hit the floor I was scared. Twenty minutes later I fell into quicksand. 'Help, help. Please help, I am stuck,' I shouted.
Finally someone pulled me out. It was over.

Ryan Silman (9)

**Snaith Primary School, Snaith**

## IN SPACE

'Bing, bang, bogle, rack,' babbled the bold aliens. With their gloomy eyes they stared straight at me. Gulp. I'd never seen anything like it. They pulled something out of their glimmering spaceship. Suddenly the pointed a weapon straight at me. 'Help! Oh no.'
Phew they missed. Would I survive?

Emily Whaley (8)

**Snaith Primary School, Snaith**

## DESERT DISASTERS

Immediately the helicopter crashed onto a sandy golden desert. Amongst the sand there were humped-back camels, lying peacefully under a tree. Oh no! Suddenly a sandstorm hit. But all the sand disappeared. The helicopter turned into a submarine. We were under the sea. Magically we both turned into dolphins.

Katie Arundale (8)

**Snaith Primary School, Snaith**

## THE HAUNTED HOUSE

*Puff!* I entered the creepy house, a gang of ghosts swayed around me. As I walked on scarlet blood dripped before my eyes. I was petrified. Suddenly the floor opened. I fell into an ebony black hole. 'It was a hidden trap!' I cried. 'Will I ever get out ... ?'

Becky Grogan (9)
**Snaith Primary School, Snaith**

## A GENIE EXPERIENCE

*Puff!* Unmistakable golden smoke immediately started to pour out of the shimmering lamp. 'Oh help it's a genie!' screamed the little girl named Ellie. 'I wish you would disappear. Mummy's going to flip!'
Another puff went off! Angrily, the genie emerged back into the lamp. Would Genie forgive Ellie's reactions?

Megan Jeffery (9)
**Snaith Primary School, Snaith**

## THE HAUNTED HOUSE

*Thump, thump!* What was that? Silence struck. There, I heard it again! There on the grass was scarlet red blood! It was like murder! Argh! The door was creaking! I went inside. There was nothing there until ... a ghost appeared! Was I sleeping? Someone pinch me! Was this true?

Katherine Barr (7)

**Snaith Primary School, Snaith**

## THE DUNGEON

*Whoosh!* The creaky door swooped open. *Bang!* It bounced straight back at me! I stuck my hand out in shock. It creaked again. I slowly crept forwards in horror. Goblins and ghouls stood there before me. I walked. As I got closer, sights became clearer. Would I get their gold?

Kian Denton (8)

**Snaith Primary School, Snaith**

## FOOLISH WITCH'S ADVENTURE

*Zoom!* Foolish witch's broomstick took off. 'Argh!' screeched Foolish witch at the top of her high-pitched voice. 'My broom is uncontrollable,' screamed the witch. The helpless witch couldn't control her broom. Her friend, Billy the wizard, came. He said, 'No,' to her problem. Would she ever escape?

Erin Simpson (9)

**Snaith Primary School, Snaith**

## ATTACK OF THE SLITHEEN

'Where are we going next Doctor?'
'Nowhere, we're not going anywhere until you get out of the TARDIS.'
'Alright.' Suddenly the TARDIS made a weird noise and went dark red. 'Where are we?'
*Roar.* There in front stood a Slitheen.
'Run, quick, it will kill you if you stay here!'

Finlay Butler (9)

**Snaith Primary School, Snaith**

## THE DISAPPEARING WITCH

With a puff of smoke a magical witch came out of nowhere and looked in an unusual book of spells. She was practising her magical spells. 'Alacazam, alicazoom, turn my cat into a donkey.' *Whoosh!* She turned into the donkey instead! Do you think she will come back?

Abbie Riley (8)

**Snaith Primary School, Snaith**

## THE SPOOKY DEVIL

*Slam!* The creepy devil tiptoed across the creaky floorboards. *Creak!*

It was so silent you could hear a pin drop. Immediately the door flung open once more and everybody around the village was petrified. People were shaking. Oh no! Will the villagers survive? *Gosh!* That was a nightmare.

Scott Robinson (8)

**Snaith Primary School, Snaith**

## THE MUSEUM

'Wow Mum, I love it!' Happily I stared into the glass. My mum didn't reply. Then I realised my mum was a cave woman. They glared into my eyes as I backed away slowly. I heard a soft yet evil voice saying, 'I'm coming, we're coming.' They broke the glass!

Kyra-Mae MacKinnon (8)

**Snaith Primary School, Snaith**

## THE DEMON DINNER LADY

The demon dinner lady plunged out her hand. She viciously grabbed the scrumptious chocolate cake of mine and elatedly stuffed the cake, gloopy and delicious, into her mouth. While she was eating the wonderful mixture of the chocolate cake, you could see the horrible wart on her. The horrible maggot.

Caitlin Tate (8)

**Snaith Primary School, Snaith**

## THE SHIVER UP MY SPINE ... SLAM!

*Slam!* The doors firmly shut. I felt something wet on my shoulder. Rapidly, I turned to find live goo! I stood and stared. I got a strange feeling, then I got a shiver up my spine. Zombies appeared then skeletons. Suddenly I realised I was being captured. Would I survive ... ?

Lauren Selkirk (8)
**Snaith Primary School, Snaith**

## UNTITLED

*Clank! Twonk!* went the spanner. Doctor Van Helsing (the inventor) spent his whole life trying to perfect his invention, a colossal robot. Now let's test it. Which button is the on button? He pressed a big red button - unexpectedly, a buzz sound occurred. 'Huh?' mumbled the inventor, 'It's not working.'

Matthew Bean (9)
**Snaith Primary School, Snaith**

## THE MOULDY BEANS

I put some warm beans in the freezing fridge. But I left the boiling beans in for too long. I put them in on Monday, now it was Sunday. I only realised it was Sunday because I had my Sunday socks on. I found my beans and they were mouldy.

Ryan Knowles (9)

**Snaith Primary School, Snaith**

## THE HOLE OF MYSTERY

*Splash!* Water splashed out of the neat yellow painted wall. 'Argh!' I screamed suddenly. Glistening blood whooshed out of a hole in the wall. But where did the hole come from? Did I just notice it or was it already there? 'Hmm,' I murmured, puzzled. What should I do?

Lauren Johnston (8)

**Snaith Primary School, Snaith**

## CONFUSED FROG

Confused, the frog, was very bewildered! Confusingly, Confused, the frog, was allergic to water! One fine day, Confused decided to jump to New York City and he lived in London! When he was there all he saw was bright flashing lights and water. He needed to get out, but how?

Ellie Hamilton (8)
**Snaith Primary School, Snaith**

## THE DOG THAT LIKED TO DIG

Once there was a dog, a hound dog to be exact. He loved to dig. One day he went to dig up a bone that he'd hidden. So he dug but found nothing so he tried again, found a whole pile of bones. Giant skeleton dinosaur bones. *Yummy, yummy, yum.*

Luke Couch (8)
**Snaith Primary School, Snaith**

## UNTITLED

The first rocket that was going to explore the whole galaxy had set off with eight passengers. Unfortunately when they got to Uranus a black hole had sucked them up. The passengers thought they were doomed, but they did not die. Instead, they saw a massive spaceship approaching them.

Ashwath Hari (10)
**Stone Cross School, Pevensey**

## THE THREE LITTLE PIGS

One day three pigs left home, they went to get their own homes. One was made of straw, another, twigs and then the last one, bricks. A wolf blew them all down except the one made of bricks and everyone lived in there, except the wolf. The wolf died.

Maddison Burgess (10)
**Stone Cross School, Pevensey**

## CRAZY CHRISTMAS!

Sophie woke up in the night, hearing a bang coming from the kitchen. It stopped and started again, so she went downstairs and there they were in front of her. The Christmas lights on, presents around it. Pink and purple, green and blue, stripy and spotty, Father Christmas had been!

Hannah Ginno (10)
**Stone Cross School, Pevensey**

## GHOSTLY GOINGS-ON

Stacey walked into the kitchen to make a cup of soup, the door slammed. A bloodsucking vampire appeared before her wide opened eyes. Stacey attempted to make a quick exit but the vampire pulled her back, opening his mouth ready for his dinner. Yuck!

Charlotte Williams (10)
**Stone Cross School, Pevensey**

## THE ALIENS ATTACK TOP GEAR

Top Gear got attacked by aliens in a Reliant Robin. The star in the reasonably priced car accelerated hard and squished the aliens. The star stepped out, he was Doctor Who. Jeremy was very pleased. Jeremy announced the top of the leaderboard for squishing aliens is Doctor Who. Good night!

Nathan Croft (10)

**Stone Cross School, Pevensey**

## SINISTER SAUSAGE SAGA

A sinister battle took place at the beginning of time. Zeus, Poseidon and Hades were brothers. Zeus attacked Poseidon with lightning. Poseidon fought back with a tidal wave. Hades joined in, riding around in his Goth black chariot. All this violence just because Poseidon ate the last sausage at breakfast.

Harry Pearson (10)

**Stone Cross School, Pevensey**

## JAMES BOND'S FIRST MISSION

James Bond had just been assigned to his first mission. His satnav read unknown destination.
It was a windy night as James floored his Aston Martin Vanquish. He pulled into the nearly deserted car park, walked slowly into the building and purchased a six-pack of Carlsberg for the queen!

Alfie Travers (10)

**Stone Cross School, Pevensey**

## THE UNDISCOVERED GOLDMINE

One day my friend and I went to the park. After half and hour we were on the swings. All of a sudden a big hole shot through the earth and a goldmine appeared, so we jumped down the hole and there was a whole new world discovered.

George Warris (9)

**The Hermitge Junior School, Woking**

## THE NAUGHTY SHARK

One day a fish was swimming in the sea, when he bumped into Naughty Shark. The fish tried to swim away, but Naughty Shark was too fast. *Gulp!* Fish had gone.

Sam Rawson (9)
**The Hermitge Junior School, Woking**

## BELLA'S BUBBLE BOX

One Monday morning at school Jenny saw a big, sparkling box. She rushed out of her seat to open the box. When opened, millions of bubbles flew out. When they popped a fairy called Bella appeared and granted Jenny a special wish. It can only be used when she's sad.

Bethany Edwards (9)
**The Hermitge Junior School, Woking**

## SUPER HERO DREAMS!

At last, it was their day off! JD and Sparky were relaxing at home, when ... *flash, bang!* A red streak of lightning whizzed across the sky. Oh no ... Rico the evil green alien bunny was at large again!
'Sparky, Sparky, wake up, don't you want to go for a walkie?'

Ryan Fayers (9)
**The Hermitge Junior School, Woking**

## THE FLOWERBED DEFEATS THE PIES

Pies started to emerge from the ground! Jack ran into his house, but the pies tried to get in! Luckily what the pies didn't know was that Jack had planted some plants, which would somehow defeat the pies and heroically save his friends and his own life. Hip hip hooray!

Jack Donovan (10)
**The Hermitge Junior School, Woking**

## THE UNDERWORLD

The bang was so loud. The life was drained from my body. The moment I saw it I was scared. I saw the underworld. It was horrid, there were monsters and zombies. That moment I woke up, away from that horrid place. But it will haunt me. The underworld.

Peter Beech (11)
**The Hermitge Junior School, Woking**

## TWISAL THE SUPER RABBIT

Twisal found a hole in the field. He went inside and investigated. He saw a three-eyed rabbit called Fang. 'I'm going to trap you in glass.' Fang grabbed Twisal and pushed him in a bubble. Twisal had super mint and rubbed it on the glass. It broke - Twisal escaped.

Alexandra Rayner (8)
**The Hermitge Junior School, Woking**

## WAS IT A DREAM?

I imagined it would be normal when I woke, but I saw a fairy. She went downstairs so I decided to follow her into the kitchen. She gave me a blue wand then sprinkled multicoloured dust on me. Suddenly ... I was in my bed! Was it a dream?

Shanice Simpson (10)
**The Hermitge Junior School, Woking**

## THE MERMAID

A girl about nine years old was wandering along the rocks when suddenly she fell in. She started to cough and splutter because she could not swim. But she found that she could, she stared at her legs, she had a tail. She realised that she was a beautiful mermaid.

Ellen Stone (9)
**The Hermitge Junior School, Woking**

## MISSED PENALTY

Rhys went to the World Cup, it was really hot. Iniesta tried to score a penalty in the final minute but Rhys was the best goalkeeper. He jumped to the left and saved it. The crowd went wild. England had won the World Cup. They were so happy.

Rhys Gay (8)
**The Hermitge Junior School, Woking**

## IN THE SPOTLIGHT

One day Laura saw a dancer on TV. Laura wanted to be like her so she went to the shops and bought a tutu, ballet shoes and hair pins. Off Laura went to ballet. She was the best in her class and she performed in the school of ballet performance.

Sarah Coxon (9)
**The Hermitge Junior School, Woking**

## UNDERWATER ADVENTURE

'Let's go diving,' said Scarlett.
'OK,' said Tom. 'Argh!' We've got tails,' they shouted, 'we're mermaids. Let's swim around the sea and look for shells.' They swam around and found a shark swimming towards them. 'Swim away.' They are at the beach again. 'Never go underwater again,' puffed Tom.

Phoebe Fishlock (9)

**The Hermitge Junior School, Woking**

## THE DIARY

When Jodie was strolling to class she spotted Hannah. Jodie raced over to Hannah and bullied her! When Jodie got home, she wrote in her diary how she couldn't stop bullying Hannah. That next morning Jodie's diary had written and told her what to do! Then they were BFFS!

Hattie Collyer (9)

**The Hermitge Junior School, Woking**

## MELTING IGLOO!

The penguin started to build his igloo. Then he thought it was getting hot. So he went inside his igloo. He looked outside, the sun was there , his igloo melted so he had to build another one. It never got hot again except in the summer!

Laura Tweedie (9)

**The Hermitge Junior School, Woking**

## THE GREEN ALIEN!

Blobby was a green alien who had a human mother. He looked human until he was five and Mum discovered his secret. She shoved him outside. Blobby was sad but his mum really loved him and invited him back for a birthday surprise.

Fiona Stalker (9)

**The Hermitge Junior School, Woking**

## GREAT SPACE EXPLORATION!

There once was a girl who longed to visit the stars! One day she won a competition and the prize was a space adventure to the stars! Her dream came true! She was overjoyed! She wrote everything in her diary so she'd never forget her great time in outer space.

Shruti Attarde (10)

**The Hermitge Junior School, Woking**

## THE WOOD

I was alone in the deep, dark wood. Although it was light outside, the trees were so tall they blocked out the sun. I heard a crunching in the leaves and birds flying away. The crunching got louder and louder until ... Oh, thank goodness, it was just a ravenous rabbit!

Amira Bhatt (9)

**Tudor Primary School, Finchley**

## HOPE

In the bleak mid-winter, the wind moaned through the trembling trees. The earth was hard as iron and the water turned to stone. A special boy came into the garden. Ice melted; doves flew through the apple blossom; mothers sang lullabies. He looked around and smiled.

Anjali Jadav (9)
**Tudor Primary School, Finchley**

## WHAT A DAY!

Alice and her dad went to the fair. Alice saw a rainbow of colours, bright balloons, jazzy music and she could smell candyfloss and burnt toffee apples. Her dad bought her a porcelain doll with flaxen hair. Dad hit a bull's eye! That night, she dreamt of her perfect day.

Sonal Shah (9)
**Tudor Primary School, Finchley**

## A SPECIAL LION

One day in the African Savannah, a very special lion cub was born. His name was Simba and he was destined to become king of the pride. However, his uncle had been rejected from the animal kingdom. Brooding, malevolent and in despair, he plotted to kill Simba. He failed.

Ayah Daniel-Rashid (9)
**Tudor Primary School, Finchley**

## DONNA

Donna was a girl who liked her name. Also, she was good at maths and loved playing with her friends.

One day, her friend didn't do very well in her maths test. So Donna helped her and she did much better next time. Have you got a friend like Donna?

Donna Tabrizifar (9)
**Tudor Primary School, Finchley**

# YOUNG WRITERS INFORMATION

We hope you have enjoyed reading this book - and that you will continue to enjoy it in the coming years.

If you like reading and creative writing drop us a line, or give us a call, and we'll send you a free information pack.

Alternatively if you would like to order further copies of this book or any of our other titles, then please give us a call or log onto our website at **www.youngwriters.co.uk**

Young Writers Information
Remus House
Coltsfoot Drive
Peterborough
PE2 9JX
Tel: (01733) 890066